FROM DAWN TO DUSK

Reminiscences of a wonderful life

Graham A. Platt

Dedicated with gratitude to the treasured
memory of my beloved – Muriel.

From Dawn to Dusk
Reminiscences of a wonderful life

ISBN 978-0-948444-59-3

First published in 2012 on behalf of
Longworth and District History Society
by **Thematic Trails**,
7 Norwood Avenue, Kingston Bagpuize with Southmoor,
Oxfordshire. OX13 5AD   www.thematic-trails.org

Typing of text from original manuscript, Pam Woodward.
Text editing and proof reading by Janet Keene.
Design and lay-out by Peter Keene

Printed by Berforts Information Press, Eynsham, Oxon U.K.

Cover Illustrations

Front cover: Bluebells at Badbury Hill, near Faringdon.
Inside front cover: Grapham A. Platt. April 2012

Rear cover: My war journey. A map marking the progress of the 11th Armoured Division. Normandy June 1944 to Flensburg on the Danish border in 1945.

Inside rear cover:
Upper: Muriel amongst bluebells at Badbury Hill.
Lower: 2010 Moments after scattering Muriel's ashes.
                          Sue and Phil (husband) pause with pet dogs.
                          In Red Dell above our cottage.

CONTENTS

ILLUSTRATIONS

INTRODUCTION

It was springtime when I started writing this book at the request of relatives and friends, a request which moved inexorably towards a demand. The year has moved into a blustering Autumn. However, the sun is streaming into my front room, a room which faces to the west so making the sunlight shine comfortingly on my back whilst the sound of music fills the house gently and amicably. Perhaps I was urged to record my memories by well-meaning people in order to provide occupational therapy! You know – give the aged stroke-ridden man something to do! But, honestly, I have enjoyed performing the act of holding, in imagination, the hand of my readers to guide them through my life.

So many people in the village have helped me. To all of them, I put on record my sincere thanks, from changing my hampered handwriting into type-written sheets, to guiding those sheets into printed illustrated form, all done in the capable, experienced hands of the Local History Society. My thanks too for so many photos included in this book. My apologies to those, now unknown and unacknowledged, photographers who in past years have caught moments of my life, printed herein to help record so many treasures!

One daughter and some grandchildren luckily live a few miles away to help me. Added to this, I am so fortunate to be surrounded in this village by so many who ensure that I'm still alive and healthy in mind and body. To all, thank you!

Now, take hold of my hand and let me guide you through my life, from 1920 to the present day.

Kingston Bagpuize with Southmoor, Autumn, 2011.

PROLOGUE

I should not really be here! Yet, here I am, pen in hand, alive – alone, sitting in silence, gazing outside across the fields at trees, now standing bare-branched in February sun, long winter-dormant but waiting, gently stirring to waken and spread their branches, leaf-bursting into their hundredth summer growth. How many hundred more will they endure?

I should not really be here! Yet here I am in my ninety-second year, with my pen and my memories, my inward eye which I know to be my "bliss of solitude". All my years have been spent with golden bursts of treasures and of wonders. "I must remember this!" I would cry, and store the golden moment safely.

There have been moments of sheer terror, life-threatening bolts of red-black danger. If I had moved this way not that, but as I have said, and repeat, I should not really be here. But I am! Let me guide you – as best I may – and you can join me as I open for you my treasure chest of golden, and sometimes leaden, moments stored within.

Graham A. Platt

1. BIRTH AND EARLIEST MEMORIES

To begin the journey, I take you back to New Year's Day, 1920, when I was born. I cannot, dare not, presume that to have been a treasured memory. The earliest chunk of gold was when I was probably two years old, standing by the large sash-window of the playroom – a room bare of any furniture. One large cupboard stored toys, small chairs and books. But the window held my child-like thoughts. Rain was making rambling raindrop races. The sky was overcast. No sign of any late brightness, just persistent rain. I could not understand it. I knew that it was Sunday. My father's large drapery store was closed. But Sunday! The very name seemed wrong. Alone in the room, I said aloud to the room's ears, "This is my first wet Sunday!" It was locked into my treasure chest and is there for eternity'

Surely I'm not alone – the only person with such early treasured thoughts. I had an early wilfulness, determination, a mindfulness of justice and care. In hospital recovering from a double hernia operation (made necessary after developing a serious cough caught from my nurse) I tolerated the hospital food. But toleration gave way to boredom when I realized that stewed apple was the one and only dessert. I recall saying to my cot's ears only, "If it is stewed apple again today, I shall throw it out of my cot!"

It was a promise. It arrived. It was. I did. And I felt a pleasure in carrying out my promise. The pleasure dimmed slightly on my mother's arrival that afternoon. I can see her now, sweeping majestically into the ward, smiling then pausing to chat to a nurse, "And how is he today?"

The memory fades. I cannot recall any stern words, just love and concern. However, the treasure chest opened, and closed quietly. I remember recovering at home playing on the fireside rug with my brothers, my mother seated watching us with toys surrounding her three boys but I sat on mine guarding them with nappy-cushioned comfort. When my brothers asked for some building object held beneath me I refused. "My dear," said my mother, "you must learn to share!" I, wisely, obeyed!

Although small and, I suppose, a weak child, I was always thinking of growing in height. I well remember the day that I stood by the dining room table laid ready for a meal. I stood alone by the table's edge, at probably the age of 2 or 3 years and said to no-one but myself, "At last I can see the table." as I gazed at the surface of the cloth, plates and cutlery. I was able to look upon it all with satisfaction and sense of achievement! I was growing taller!

Mother and 3 children. Gordon 3, Me 1½, Landon 6

2. BROTHERLY GAMES AND FIRST FORMAL SCHOOLING

Growing up, the youngest of three boys, was full of games in the playroom – blackboard, easel, desks, chalk – eldest the Headmaster, middle one the teacher, and me, the youngest, the pupil!

Starting school at the age of five was easy – I could read, write and had a sense of numbers. I was moved quickly to the next class – a room so large it seemed to hold about fifty pupils. I was given the only spare seat available and quickly realized all children were seated according to ability – and I was at a desk at the bottom of the class. So I assumed the cloak of a dunce. The next day the absentee returned to his seat so I was moved to the next available desk – at the top of the class. I said to the desk's ears, "Now I'm clever." and I put on a different cloak and stayed like that until father moved us all to the seaside. And why was that? I must tell you that while I was clever, I was small of size, a weakling. Some years later I heard my parents talking about the move – a move which required my father to travel up to London daily to see to his shops. I heard my mother say quietly, with a nod of her head in my direction, "Well it was that he might live." Those words amazed me. A special drawer of the chest shot open and slid back gently and quietly. I told you I should not really be here!

But, back to the early twenties.
Having found it easy to read and write, my mother fed my imagination and my emotions by reading fairy tales to me at the age of probably four cuddled together by the fireside. I remember so well 'The Little Match Girl' me feeling warm, secure, cosy, loved, but imagining the poor cold lonely little girl selling her matches at the kerbside and me, realizing the inevitable ending, burst into sobs crying out to my mother to stop reading on and on to the awful end.

3. BOOKS, CINEMA AND THEATRE

Mother would take the three of us to the local cinema close to father's shops. I watched the silent flickering screen with amazement. After a few visits my mother said, "You must read the speeches for yourself now. I'm not going to help you."

I was wisely thrown in at the literary deep end and I swam, swam, swam through comedy, horror, love and drama with the likes of Mary Pickford, Harold Lloyd, Rudolph Valentino, Charlie Chaplin.

My father tolerated this modern technology of the 1920s but quietly disapproved. He loved the theatre and every Thursday, being half-closing day, after his visit to the City for ordering stock, we were always taken, all five, full family to the nearby theatre where we saw the wonders of music hall – George Robey, Nellie Wallace, the Houston Sisters, Harry Tate – so many of the great performers of that period – who would move from theatre to theatre to slot into each theatre-timed turn, first house or second house.

I know my mother revelled in these visits. Her maiden name was Pounds and her cousins were among those music hall artistes – Lorna and Toots Pounds, Curtis Pounds.

I enjoyed every visit, every performance. The interval might have made me impatient but the ever thoughtful Mother always had the answer. The safety curtain would by law be lowered at that moment, a curtain full of advertisements, a miraculous opportunity for the game of 'I-Spy'. Mother would start the game. "I spy with my little eye the word 'Shoes'." Our quick search followed to find and read out the whole advertisement. Learning has been always such enjoyment – with fun, laughter mingled with deep feelings as new experiences pour into the young brain.

Later, as you will recall, was the move away from that familiar fire-side, happy playroom, the slope of wood on the landing, a three-foot slope from one level to another. My brothers and I would slide from top to bottom, a length of about eight feet. We called it our "Slip, slop, slorum". Strange, lovely, happy name. "Let's play on our slip, slop, slorum!" we would cry out. Is it there still? If so does the air round it still ring to the sound of treble voices?

On walks with my brothers at that time, we would pause to look at manhole covers. We imagined evil monsters lurking beneath these covers. We would stamp our feet on them to keep the horrors from heaving them up. There was a strange name we gave them – now what was it? Never written, just spoken! It was the feared Big Oggean!

I have moved you back and forth through these early years, opening and closing this wild, weird chest of my mind. So much keeps urging me to let something fly out to amuse you! Such as our maids who came and went into and out of our three little minds. Mother would interview a newcomer and once I was able to overhear the conversation. "Yes, my dear," my mother said, "you may start tomorrow. But one thing, what is your Christian name?" An answer came, I forget the unnecessary detail. "Oh, that won't do," my mother said firmly, "we shall call you Annie. I make that a rule. It's so much easier for my children." You see, our first maid was Annie, so all the followers had to be "re-Christened" on arrival! Dear Mother, always scheming to ease us into the complicated, fragile world, one so recently shattered by the slaughter of World War I. It was a world in which, in those early years, the few men I saw around had so

The three brothers
Me aged 8, Gordon aged 10, Landon aged 13

many limbs missing. I knew not how many whole bodies had shattered minds. I knew not as I grew up into my teenage years how I, too, would be deeply affected by cruel sights in yet another world war.

Yes, you must see with me some nightmare horrors as I permit those dark-panelled, deep cupboard doors to open with un-oiled screams of protest. Oh, memory hold the door for now. Keep closed till later.

For now, happy, laughing, sunlit schooldays by the sea, in a newly built large house surrounded in those early years by fields.

I recall one sunny summer day, my brothers and I were sitting at the table for lunch in the kitchen. The meal finished, Mother was in the scullery clearing the dishes. I was eating a banana. I slipped the last portion into my mouth, drew a breath at the wrong moment and started choking, unable to lodge the fruit safely to my stomach. The strangled noise of my attempts to breath was very weird indeed. My brothers started laughing not realizing the seriousness of the occasion. My mother heard the disturbance, dashed in, dragged me out, through the kitchen to the open back door and thumped me hard on the back of my neck. My stomach received the piece of banana safely. Mother took me back to the table whilst berating my poor brothers. But all was well. I lived. Hints of what if?

Other times, after lunch, years later, Mother would sit in her easy chair in the kitchen – later to become the morning room for breakfast – whilst the three of us did clearing: washing up done by the eldest, the drying by the middle one, round the doorway and to the enormous cupboard, the one to put things away, me the youngest.

Mother sat in her chair murmuring quietly, "Do be careful boys!" because eldest threw a wet plate to be dried, job done middle one threw the dry plate round the corner, caught by me to put it in its correct place in the cupboard. It was speed of action, good eye for catching, laughter and enjoyment without any breakages and our cries of, "Don't worry, Mother!"

Happy, wonderful days to treasure!

4. SEASIDE AND DEEPER THOUGHTS

The three of us would walk out each morning at 8.15! A happy ritual!

"Quick boys! The ten-past-eight-man has just gone by." - about the man hurrying by towards the little railway station for the next London train.

"Hymn books, prayer books, Bibles?" she asked. Hymn books, yes, we each had our own, but "prayer books and Bible" really meant "Homework all done and packed in your satchels." We understood the ever-repeated reminder and off to enjoy the next glorious day of soaking up knowledge. It was a private boys' school – boarders and day boys; the school later to be granted public school status. We all did well, gaining class book prizes at the annual Speech Days. Many of these still nestle happily on my shelves sleeping quietly amongst all my later literary joys.

Langorham, 60 Mount Avenue, Westcliff-on-Sea.
Built in 1927. Garage added later

Me aged eight in garden at Westcliff

Class sizes at that school were reasonably small – about 20 to 25 pupils. The age range was six to eighteen. I started at the age of seven in the preparatory department, a house separated from the main building, where the tuition was very modern for that day. For example, we were often at that early age made to take part in a well-constructed debating society. I revelled in that when made to chair and keep in order the proceedings. Speech and communication was uppermost all the time. Correct use of the English language spoken and written was paramount at all times. Yes, elocution was part of the curriculum, together with the art of writing.

We had to give short talks to the class on any subject demanded by the teacher. Later, as we grew older, we had to give a mini-lecture to the school at morning assembly. The first I gave was, I remember, on the subject of Time and the mystery of the past, fleeting present and unknown future. "But," I said, "was the future unknown completely?" I recounted to the school an incident which I had experienced a few days beforehand.

I explained how, whilst walking home from school one afternoon I saw a man walking up the slight hill towards me. I said to myself, "This man is going to ask me the time, and I have my pocket watch in the top pocket of my school blazer." I remember the road and the exact location in Crowstone Avenue. He neared me on the pavement on my left-hand side and paused. I stopped and looked at him. "Excuse me," he said politely, "but can you tell me the time, please."

I pulled out my watch, told him. He thanked me and we parted – he up the hill, me down the hill, thinking, wondering, had I willed him to ask the question or had I ventured into the future so breaking down the barriers of time?

Looking back now, as I pour my memories onto the page, I recall two moments when my father seemed to break that barrier, too.

Firstly, during the First World War, I was told how he came rapidly from the shop into the house calling to my mother. "Quickly, throw open as many windows as you can. There's going to be a great explosion." Mother rushed quickly to do as ordered. A few minutes later the blast and the noise of an exploding mass of gunpowder in Silver Street, London. The windows shook but there was no shattering glass.

Secondly, in the Thirties, when my brother (the eldest) was up at Oxford my parents were visiting to see his college and rooms. Walking up Turl Street, my father stopped and said to my mother, "Don't worry, dear, but when we meet our boy his head will probably be bandaged!" He advanced towards them. It was. He had been knocked off his bike and sustained a minor head injury the day before. We had no telephone then and, of course, there were no mobiles in those days.

What was my dear father doing with Time in Turl Street in the Thirties? And what did I manage to do in Crowstone Avenue in the Twenties?

Subterfuge and Sin

It must have been in the early thirties that my brothers and I experienced our mother's careful, gentle subterfuge to shield us from a sinful world.

Mother had had a double operation for hernia and appendicitis at a local nursing home. Realizing that recovery time at home would need help, my parents employed a maid full time, sleeping in and having her meals in the kitchen, a person apart, as befitted a "downstairs employee".

Our mother, with the help of an aunt who stayed for a little while, recovered well from what was then considered a serious operation. The maid stayed, happily working for our parents.

One day Mother happened to mention to us that she suspected the maid's honesty and that she needed to prove it. One afternoon before our usual walk down to the beach we sat round the dining-room table watching Mother count the sugar lumps out of the silver bowl on the table laid ready for tea-time. We all noted the number and left to get ready to go out for a few hours.

On our return, Mother counted the lumps – an enormous number were missing. "That's it", my mother said. "She must go". We nodded, amazed and agreed.

Some days later, we were assembled in the hall with our parents to say goodbye to the maid, case packed and weeping. "Please let me stay," she begged.

"No, dear!" said my mother, adding gently, sympathetically. "You see at this time of your life you should be with your mother!"

The poor girl had befriended a fellow she had met some weeks ago and had even entertained for tea, with permission, in her kitchen, and she was pregnant. All this we learnt later and that Dad had given her extra money and paid her fare home. She had been a cheerful jolly soul whom I liked.

Oh, there is so much more to tell you. I find it hard to find the answer to this strangeness. But back to those happy, carefree school days.

Fun and growing up

Language work – English, French, Latin – I enjoyed it all. Latin with amo, amas, amat, laudo, laudas, laudat, dominus, domine, dominum – it all made my mind think of our "slip, slop, slorum". It was all a glorious game.

Arithmetic, algebra, Euclidean geometry. I loved the solving of the riders, the puzzles. Even multiplication tables were fun. I recall one of the mistresses – plump, rounded, pleasant, Yorkshire lady making us all roll around with laughter.

> "Eight eights are sixty-four.
> Shut your gob and say no more!"

She laughed with us and when we talked to her about the Yorkshire dialect, she gave us a splendid example:

"Oppen yer gob an' show 'em yer loregar." (Open your mouth and show me your tongue). Oh, learning can and should be all so much fun.

A computer can give you facts, answers, e-mails. A mobile can give you texts (and so much more now) but neither computers nor mobiles can surround us with friendly, co-joined laughter that makes the trees sway in dance and the flowers to burst out in colourful admiration. But I must turn the pages for we have far to travel.

The Thirties moved swiftly on. Sport – tennis, badminton, swimming – I grew into disturbing manhood. I would wake up feeling different, growing from my diminutive three feet rapidly towards the eventual six feet. I would look at myself in the wardrobe mirror and cry out, "Is that really me?" Yes, it was disturbing. The voice, from treble, cracked towards a deep tenor sound. Going into shops to ask for something was nothing short of frightening. What person would leap from my mouth? Gradually, I matured – uneasily at first but then more and more into someone I could know to be me.

5. WORK, LONDON, MUSIC AND FILM

It was in 1938 that I started my first day of working life. This was at the large, well-known bookshop in Charing Cross Road straddling both sides of Manette Street. I started in the Music and Drama department, moved to the Art Department and then to the ground floor showroom where the notice at the entrance informed the public that "ici on parle français". And I did, too! But it enabled me to meet the famous authors and the stars of theatreland.

During my lunch hour I would hurry down to the National Gallery to pay an entrance fee of one shilling (10p) to the short piano recitals. There I sat entranced by the magical playing of Myra Hess. Music was beginning to fill my life.

21

I must wind back the reel of memory three or four years. Forgive me – but this is important. I was tuning in the Pye radio (wireless!) at 5.15 for the commencement of Children's Hour and the beginning of an historical play by L. du Garde Peach.   Music burst out from the loudspeaker, an urgent, fateful, melodramatic fanfare. My ears were shattered. I gasped with amazement. What incredible sound! It was the opening of the first movement of Tchaikovsky's 4th Symphony.   I was emotionally hooked. The play was forgotten but those first few bars of music were stored forever.

My very first attendance for a full orchestral concert was one evening at the Queen's Hall, Langham Place.   I bought a programme. I still have it.

The date was Monday, 22th May 1939. The seventh in a series of Beethoven concerts. The orchestra was the BBC Symphony Orchestra.

The works played were to start with two movements of Beethoven's String Quartet in F, the No. 3 Overture Leonora and ending with Beethoven's Ninth Symphony (the Choral) and the conductor was Arturo Toscanini. Soloists included Isobel Baillie and Margaret Balfour.

At the start, the immediate sound, the live sound of the full orchestra sent shivers down my spine, the hairs of my scalp to trembling with emotion.

Toscanini, small of stature, conducted throughout without a score, in complete control, growing in stature and musical energy until the great ending of Beethoven's 9th.

As the last chords roared over me triumphantly, I sat exhausted as the audience stood and roared. How I managed to walk away that night, to reach my railway station, to get off at the right station, to walk the short distance to my parents' home, where they, too, had heard the concert on the radio, but not live, not with me in the concert hall where I had experienced that overwhelming reality, my top-drawer golden award-winning treasure. Below; title page of my programme.

Queen's Hall

SEVENTH

Beethoven Concert

Monday 22 May 1939 at 8.15 p.m.

Adagio and Andante quasi Allegretto
(Prometheus Ballet Music) (Op. 43)

Lento assai and Vivace (String Quartet in F, Op. 135)

Overture Leonora No. 3 (Op. 72a)

INTERVAL

Symphony No. 9, in D minor (Choral) (Op. 125)

Isobel Baillie   Margaret Balfour
Parry Jones   Harold Williams
The BBC Choral Society

(Chorus Master : Leslie Woodgate)

The BBC Symphony Orchestra

Leader: Paul Beard   Organ: Berkeley Mason

CONDUCTOR : # Arturo Toscanini

*The Concert will be broadcast from 8.15 p.m. to 10.30 p.m. with an interval
from 9 p.m. to 9.20 p.m. approx.*

23

I filled those days and months in London with music, theatre, films many of them French – Un Carnet de Bal, Quai des Brumes, La Kermesse Héroïque. But there was one English film which I saw one afternoon at the Empire Cinema in Leicester Square. I had bought a ticket for the cheapest seat right high in the balcony area, looking down at the small screen watching "Goodbye Mr. Chips". Tears were in my eyes throughout. I wanted to cry out with repressed emotion and longing. I knew so well what I longed to be. I wanted to teach children, to help them to find the joy of the world around them, to share my enthusiasm for the beauty of all the arts and for knowledge and truth. I wanted to teach them all this – but it was 1939.

One evening I was on the bus taking me from Charing Cross Road to Fenchurch Street Station.

A charming, well-dressed lady of mature years passed me to gain her seat. She paused as she passed me, looked at me, smiled gently, but as she sat down she turned to look at me – a young twenty year old. The smile had vanished. She turned away and started weeping. People turned but kept quiet. She moved to get off the bus at a stop before Fenchurch Street, paused still weeping, in front of me. I put a hand up to help her as the bus braked. She grasped it, looked into my eyes, gently squeezed my hand, let go, and weeping left my world. The bus moved off, other passengers having witnessed the scene, were silent. I was left bewildered but have since wondered. Had she lost a son, a husband, a lover in the First World War? Was she reminded of her loss, her grief and feared for the youth in 1939, as storm clouds had gathered over the then-called Czechoslovakia and the threat of the invasion of Poland?

6. FROM PEACE TO WAR

The invasion came and with it a declaration of war together with my call-up papers! No longer was I free to travel up to London to enjoy the arts, to obey my father's warning not to join in card games with dishonest, cheating travellers. To heed my mother's warning about women of disease-ridden ill-repute. I was about to be thrown, hurled into the society of a world of young men, some who shared my thinking and language but many who had had a childhood upbringing in what was to me another culture, another language – to me another planet! My public school education had not warned me.

Perhaps it was this that my caring headmaster was warning me about. My brother – the eldest – had gone up to Oxford gained a degree in modern languages and Diploma of Education to take up teaching French at a private boarding school. Our father had said he could only afford to send one of us to University but, in touching fairness had told us that in his Will he intended to divide his estate between the three of us evenly except for the reduction of the eldest's share by the full cost of his years at Oxford.

That satisfied us all but when I reached the age of fifteen my headmaster suggested I should work hard towards aiming at a scholarship to Oxford. Chatting to my then undergraduate brother, he warned me that scholars up at Oxford had to wear, in those days, a scholar's gown and they were regarded by many as outcasts and to be shunned. Life would be miserable. I worked at my studies but never tried for a scholarship. When my Headmaster questioned me about my thoughts of a career I mentioned teaching. His only thoughts were university and teaching in private or public schools, thinking I would be miserable in State education. It was the care and protection of the class system of his day.

Yes, in those days, it was strong, it existed. I recall Mother got us together one day in the lovely rooms of our new house by the sea and said, "Remember this, my boys, you are middle class, not upper class, nor working class. You are middle class."

No wonder then, quiet, caring Headmaster, loving, adored parents, little did you all realize or give dire warning of the culture shock the weak-not-expected-to-live seven year old that had become the six-foot, twenty-year-old was to experience in August 1940.

First Days of Army life

I was thrown into close contact, rubbing shoulders with some young men whose language contained short sentences blurted out with strange adjectival limitation. All things were effing good, effing bad, effing this and effing that. I lived with them, laughed with them, suffered the learning of army discipline and drill but maintained my own use of the English language with loving, laughing care. I got to know them all; they in turn respected me as a colleague but a few of them were to become close friends. As new recruits in a newly arrived squad we survived those weeks of training as gunners-to-be for artillery regiments.

On our arrival at Dover Castle the first shells from the German heavy artillery were fired across the Channel. The evacuation from Dunkerque had occurred some weeks before. We, in Dover Castle, were really front line troops with the few miles of water between us and the enemy! Barrage balloons hung in the sunshine above the old ramparts and the buildings which housed our dormitory.

To underline the crass stupidity of our posting to Dover Castle we were awakened a few days after our arrival by the sound of a trumpet call. A sergeant burst in and ordered us to get up at once to dress in our new unaccustomed uniform. The sergeant explained that the trumpet call was an urgent rhythmic warning. "Learn that call. It means 'There's a Jerry in the camp' repeated and repeated. Come and follow me quickly." We were taken into a stone walled, badly lit room. In walked an army major, portly, round, grey moustached face.

"Men," he boomed staring round at us, "the invasion may come tonight!" And he continued to say we must defend the castle and follow all orders. It seemed to me like some incredible, overacted comedy, even farce. Out we went into the night, being led to various parts of the castle. We reached the East Gate, paused as our guide, the sergeant, looked round. His eyes landed on me. He opened a crate and lifted out what looked to me like a metal ball.

"Have you ever seen these?" he asked. I shook my head. "Well, it's a hand grenade. You see this pin with the small ring at the end?" I nodded in silence. "You put your finger in that ring and pull the pin out. If any of the enemy come up that roadway," he pointed out through the tunnel leading out to the east, "you just throw that grenade at them. Right?" I nodded, struck silent in dumb amazement.

I held the grenade in my hand, watched the sergeant stride off with the rest of the squad.

It was about midnight. I sat down. I looked at the open roadway leading out to dimly visible fields beyond. Nobody came. All was peaceful. Alone I was defending the castle, saving the country, with one hand grenade. But nothing, nobody came until five in the morning. A one-stripe, a lance bombardier told me "False alarm. Stand down." He took the grenade from me and I found my way back to our billet.

Curtain. The comedy or farce was over. I often wonder now if this curious incident was the result of an awful communication mix-up somewhere off Devon (or was it Cornwall?) on some beach landing exercise. Perhaps! But that night adventure – I remember so well.

But serious training. I learned how to ride a motor bicycle – on BSA and Norton. I learnt the morse code and how to send messages by buzzer and, oh dear, by flashing lamp. Yes, lamp! Was I training for the 14-18 War, or Waterloo? How truly unprepared we all were. Line could be laid, telephones could be used. Crackling wireless communication was possible, although, as I experienced later, that could be dangerously unreliable.

Whilst still at Dover Castle, I was able to watch planes on dog-fights over the Channel; saw planes crash horribly, spectacularly with howling scream and final burst of salt-sea spray into the surface of the water; heard the whine of German fighters and the crack of machine-gun fire as they circled the ancient building puncturing the barrage balloons one by one.

Another new experience for me to store, occurred one Sunday. We had a day free of training. So four or five of us decided to attend Morning Service at the Castle church. After the service we paused outside to talk to the vicar and his wife. Suddenly, the air raid siren moaned out its warning with the immediate roar of planes and whine of bombs falling. We all fell flat, face down, hands over ears following the well-practised drill. But quite indecorously I found myself straddled over the body of the vicar's wife. Accidentally, of course, but actually unexpectedly brave and protective! Danger over, I scrambled to my feet and gently helped her up.

7. TO LANCASHIRE AND LOVE

At last, in September, we were all moved to Bamber Bridge near Preston and also, as glorious chance would have it, within reach of Bury. That move, that friend, that friend's close connection with Bury was to open up that great memory chest of my mind to receive the loveliest of jewels of my life: my love, my heart, my wife.

My friend's fiancée was friendly with a girl who was to become my wife. We all met together first in Manchester and later on in the house in Bury where I met the girl who shared my love of music, theatre, the arts, she a newly-fledged teacher, me a raw army recruit who longed to teach! We went to Manchester and Bolton to enjoy concerts by the Hallé Orchestra conducted then by Malcolm Sargent, to the theatres in Manchester. Families in the area welcomed us into their homes. We were young and alive in a world where searchlights moved their beams hither and thither across the night sky to pick out heavy droning planes ready and all too willing to drop their load of bombs.

But for us, we were young and in love. We would stroll the moors above Bury taking my love's dog Shep with us. Shep would arrive back home long before us, bored with our long pauses to kiss and kiss again. One day we went to the local shops without Shep. Walking back up the deserted side street, we were getting near the corner house which was my beloved's parents' house, I stood still. She stopped and turned towards me.

"One day, darling," I said quietly, "one day perhaps when this wretched war is over, will you, would you, dearest, become my wife?"

"Yes, yes!" No pause as she looked up to my face. "Oh, yes!" With joy, utter happiness, we kissed and kissed again, oblivious to the possibility of the twitching of many net curtains around us!
1941 when we were both twenty-one-year-old lovers!

8. TO NORTHERN IRELAND

Yes, we were young and in love. But training over, I was posted to a field artillery regiment in Northern Ireland, to Ballycarry where I was to meet more fellow soldiers who were to become my friends for life, so many who now can only exist by means of my treasure chest. They themselves and all the others that I have yet to tell you about – all now only kept alive as I pour these words out to you. Sad, yes, but oh, such happy, happy memories!

Amongst which, I recall the getting together by a sergeant who gathered six of us who could play to a high standard the game of badminton. We toured round N. Ireland challenging club after club for matches. My father had carefully wrapped up for posting my racket, complete with its press and there I was happy to represent my regiment and enjoy the sport.

I was fit and healthy. When our colonel organised a half-marathon with a prize of a free ticket to a theatre in Belfast for the first thirty runners past the tape, the whole badminton team were determined to get tickets. We did – including the once-three-feet high child not expected to live. We all went together to watch and listen to the well-known and popular George Formby. He was amusing but also unnecessarily vulgar as he obviously thought appropriate for an audience of soldiers. I found much of it offensive myself.

But exercises in and around the Sperrin Mountains and Draperstown and Lough Neagh were frequent; some just to practice the art of gunnery with 25-pounders and others with an enemy against whom we had to pretend to fight.

Once on our return in vehicles to camp thinking all was

over, we were stopped on the road and fell into an ambush. Inside our lorry we sat bemused. Our officer, seated in front, was slow to react, too. However, when an irate general and a furious brigadier roared at us all, our horrified lieutenant leapt out telling me to get out and do something. I got the others out and into a field through a gate, lay facing the gate with rifles armed at the 'enemy' whilst thunder flashes exploded amongst us.

We calmed down, stood up and listened to the general.`

Remember, in battle you are likely to be ambushed. Never just sit there waiting to be killed. Get up, fight. Do something. I am taking the vehicle away from you. You walk back to Ballycarry from here! Let that be a lesson to you all."

It was a long journey, a weary one. We had to carry all our gear which included a heavy anti-tank gun. Our officer took it off the gunner who was struggling with it.

"Give me that." he said, "That was all my fault. I'm sorry."
I admired him. He must have felt sick with his own inefficiency.

Most importantly, I have never forgotten that incident and for good reason as you will find out.

From Ireland, we moved in 1941 back to England near Doncaster. It was whilst in that area that a group of us was able to experience a visit down Askern colliery, a deep mine providing the nerve-wracking fast drop down the mineshaft, the long, dust-floored, underground roadway to the black, shiny low-ceilinged, narrow-sided working area. I knew after that the terrible working conditions, the physical back-breaking and dangerous lives that miners endure day after day. It was an experience of a side of industry, of life I had only read about in books.

But my own life as a soldier in 1941 moving into 1942 had led me first as a signaller and communication, then into work as a gunner specialist grasping the technical, mathematical side of gunnery. Part of our training was to be able to demonstrate our personal knowledge of all small arms equipment by giving a lecture on one item explaining its separate parts, its correct use and ammunition used. When it came to my turn, I was told to explain fully the Lee Enfield rifle. In front of the squad, N.C.Os and officer-in-charge, I was centre stage and in my element. Afterwards I overheard my fellow soldiers saying to each other, "Wasn't he good! I thought he was trying to sell us the blessed rifle!"

I smiled and my mind chuckled as I murmured inwardly "Satisfactory!"

I found, too, that I was being given copies of a regular booklet entitled Current Affairs and told to give talks to the battery on subjects of the day which I hoped to be truth with not too much distortion or propaganda.

One such Current Affairs booklet was a detailed analysis of the Beveridge Report. I quickly read it and gave my mini-lecture with some of the officers in the audience. A few days later the order came that all copies of the booklet were to be returned and no details of the proposals were to be mentioned or talked about. Too late! I had given and enjoyed my lecture with all its political implications! Not only that, but somehow I lost my copy of the booklet – and found it months, many months later at the bottom of my kitbag! How strange – or was it purposeful? Who knows! But I must tell you, I have it still amongst my old 1:25,000 maps of France, Belgium, Holland, Germany, so many marked with my numbering of specially prepared targets. But all those maps were to become my property years later. I must remember that I am guiding you through those early years of the 1940s.

CURRENT AFFAIRS

The Beveridge Report

ISSUED FORTNIGHTLY BY THE

ARMY BUREAU OF CURRENT AFFAIRS

Not to be Published

The information given in this publication is not to be communicated, either directly or indirectly, to the Press or to any person not holding an official position in His Majesty's Service.

No. 33   December 19th, 1942

Seven day's leave

I have already described to you, my day when I proposed to M. and how she accepted in that little street on the edge of Bury. I take you now to Worcester Park in Surrey to where my parents had moved, away from their lovely house by the Essex seashore. It was a voluntary evacuation of coastal areas, as well as movement out of London for civil service staff. All this left my uncle and aunt's house for my parents to move into temporarily.

It was near Kingston on Thames where M. and I went to buy engagement rings. Armed with our precious purchases, we went to Nonsuch Park in Cheam. Together we sat in a stone alcove looking out across the grounds. Alone. No human being in sight. Just two stone carved lions on each side of the sheltered alcove.

With rings on our fingers, solemn kisses exchanged, we sat, arms around each other. Just the two of us.

I raised my head and looked around.

"Look, darling," I murmured, "even the lions have turned their heads away."

M. looked, smiled, grinned. We laughed together to see the polite lions who sat gazing away at the lovely lawns of Nonsuch Park.

Slowly push the drawer back, turn the key, to lock that summer afternoon securely away. It was the 6th August, 1941. That number 6 appears so often! Strange! I must move you on through to the following year.

Engagement Day. Rokeby, Worcester Park, 1942.

9. BLUEBELLS AND BEYOND!

I have brought you hand in hand to the Spring of 1942. The artillery regiment had been moved to the area of Newcastle-under-Lyme in the Midlands, where, one warm evening I was walking on my own through woodland towards our camp. It was a glorious evening, sunset-shot streaks of angled light through fresh tiny leafed trees with speckled light and shade falling on swatches of bluebells making the air heavily laden with drug-filling sweetness. I stood quite still for a moment intoxicated through sight and scent. How long I stood soaking in the heavenly clothed English wood I do not remember. My legs trembled. I sank down on my knees and to the ears of that sea of blue I cried out, "Oh, God, please spare me, help me through this war to have many, many years to have this scene not only in my memory but in reality, too."

I have a book on my shelves at this moment. It is entitled 'Through the Woods'. It is by H.E. Bates and in it he describes the English woodland – April to April. It was published in 1936. I bought my copy in 1939 and wrote some personal wording on the fly-leaf. Search for it now. Read it yourself. No, no! No tears! Just clasp the treasures of life, of living as I have.

I studied and grasped the technical side of artillery work, the full use of map reading, magnetic north, grid lines, the allowance for drift, getting guns laid out on line mathematically, bracketing onto a target, the correct timing of creeping barrage, the use of the three strengths of charge (or cordite) to match distance.

With another gunner specialist we made an imitation landscape of hills, mountains, valleys, flat plains, a landscape made with hessian on a wooden frame. Underneath this large tabletop we fitted a fan-shaped

September, 1939 – War.

This book was purchased for the synthetic appreciation of Nature. The real appreciation was reluctantly stored away, only to be brought into the light in moments of quiet rest, carefree and untainted by the noise of planes, the thud of bombs or the scream of shells. Such quiet moments were few. When peace returns and nations settle down to normal quarrels, do not take such moments for granted or let them pass unnoticed. Treasure the real appreciation in Peace as you have loved the synthetic appreciation during War.

September, 1945 – Peace.

Brigham A. Pla...

Written by me to remind myself of the need to appreciate the beauty of nature

grid spreading away from an imaginary observation post. For this exercise it was just a chair placed in the large room, planned for young officers to play the game of giving orders down the line or by radio to the protected guns.

Beneath this tabletop, the two of us crouched on the floor with cigarettes alight and milk straw in hand, ready and waiting, whilst young officers were tested by a group of senior officers who gave out details of a target on the landscape to be "destroyed". As the trembling young officer barked out orders and eventually gave the order "Fire!" my colleague and I would have worked out the spot where the first shell would have landed. We would draw on the cigarette and puff the smoke up through the mesh! If the directed shell would land (on our calculation) in a hidden valley, behind a hill from the viewpoint of the O.P. one thud by one of us on the floor would mean "Explosion unsighted!"

It all sounds Heath Robinson-like, but it worked splendidly and both testers and victims appreciated the invention and the game!

I recall I had to thump time and time again for one bewildered player. He never saw a shell land and was berated by his colonel. I apologised later to him when the others had left the room and showed him where his 'shells' kept landing. He saw what he had done and we parted the best of friends.

All this led me to put forward a request to be considered for a commission. Some of the officers for whom and with whom I had worked had such a lack of leadership (and, I dare add, intelligence) that I felt sure that my bluebell prayer would be in jeopardy. Others, I envied for their ability to chat with me and sympathise, to empathise when discussing separation from a loved one, the postponement of marriage and fulfilment.

I was granted a special interview with my colonel. He listened calmly, as I explained that I felt ready to take on the responsibility of leadership.

"Good lad," he said with a smile. "First I grant you a stripe and will put forward my recommendation."

"Thank you, sir." I saluted, and from Gunner I became Lance Bombardier.

As I waited my turn for selection, I was sent on lovely courses to further my variety of talks or mini-lectures. One enjoyed above all was to Leeds University, a course based on Musical Appreciation. We each as students had to choose what work or works we would wish to lecture on. I always wanted to think of something unusual, that would possibly be seen by an 'assessor' to be different. I chose an illustrated lecture on Brahms' four symphonies. One to be considered as an imaginary 10th Beethoven Symphony leading on to the lovely 4th Symphony with its magical opening bars.

At the end the 'assessor' said, "And if you were asked by someone new to Brahms which one of the four would you advise him to start with?"

Without hesitation I replied, "Oh, number four without doubt!"

Yes, that course was a joy!

Later, with my one stripe proudly worn, I had read up the details of General Montgomery's advance from El Alamein across the desert with the sweep towards Tripoli. This success was at the time of flying bombs, intensive bombing of our cities together with the ever-present threat of invasion. I therefore made a carefully diagrammatic map explaining Monty's success with a great red curving arrow pointing round to Tripoli and pinned it up on the regimental orders board. A visiting brigadier spotted it and asked to know as he nodded approval who had done it. I heard about this after his departure and purred pleasantly!

After a few weeks I had orders to go to a place in Kent for a pre-OCTU (Officer Cadet Training Unit) Selection

Board. There a group of us, about eighteen in number were tested for intelligence, physical ability, alertness, awareness, ability to talk with confidence, ability to impress. I seemed to satisfy and, to use today's parlance, to tick all the boxes! – especially the ability to talk!

During the days there, we had several lectures on army traditions and what was expected of us when no longer in the ranks, but as officers. One of these lecturers underlined this difference in the most basic necessities of life.

"Remember this, gentlemen," he bellowed, "men shit, but officers do a rear."

Some of the gentlemen laughed. I was disturbed that such class distinction should be emphasised in such an unintelligent way.

Another day, we were each asked to give a talk on our army life so far. I remember noticing others just stood in front of their chairs to speak awkwardly. So I stood, turned and moved my chair forward and spoke behind it to gesture and embellish the tale of my experiences at Dover Castle, culminating in my lying across the vicar's wife, causing my audience, especially the selectors, to convulse with laughter. Anyway, one great leap had enabled me to jump over my first hurdle towards the goal of commissioned officer. The next move was to Catterick, Yorkshire to the gruelling months' work at the Royal Artillery Officer Cadet Training Unit.

10. CATTERICK CAMP

The barracks at Catterick were comfortable and the full course was fascinatingly programmed with time for many of us to indulge in adding to the activities.

It was there that I met the man who was to become a close friend for years. He had studied law in the Trustee Department of the Civil Service but theatre, singing and acting was his passion. Another in our group was a good pianist. The two of them arranged a concert. As they rehearsed, I was asked to listen, criticize and produce. One of his songs was Vaughan Williams' Linden Lea which he performed in strong dialect, but was anxious that each word was clear. It went well in camp hall, attended by cadets and the staff of the college.

I organised a musical appreciation group for staff workers. I recall a talk on Mozart's Symphony No. 41 – the Jupiter, detailing on blackboard all the five melodies in the last movement – introduced separately by Mozart and joined brilliantly and gloriously at the end.

Included in the long course was a period of two weeks of battle training. Our two weeks came in the month of August. We were transported in three-ton lorries with our kit to a part of England which I had never before seen. All my rural conception in childhood was flat, slightly undulating Essex.

The lorry took us to the north-eastern side of the Lake District, up a steep, snake twisting path past a tiny church, higher still, we viewed a small bungalow, nestled below a mountain surrounded by higher mountains. A tented camp was waiting for us ready to receive our kitbags. It was a glorious summer evening.

"What's that mountain?" we asked. We were told it was called The Nab.

"Right! Let's get to the top!" was the cry and off we dashed.

A long straight climb led upwards, but I decided to make the dash up through bracken and rock. I felt filled with so much joyous energy that I raced all the others and stood alone on the summit plateau. I looked to the west across what I was to know later was Ullswater with Hellvellyn beyond in blue, purple silhouetted against a yellow, red sunset merging up into a deepening blue sky.

Once more I was alone, on the top of my first mountain, fell to my knees, breathless after my climb. No prayer, just awe and wonder at the incredible glory of that landscape. My A level studies of Wordsworth, his poetry, his philosophy, his seeing God in Nature flooded over me. Alone that evening I saw the perfection of God.

I stood up. My close friend arrived next.

"Goodness, Gra," he gasped, "you must be fit!"

I smiled and we descended, they back down the long grassy slope, me alone through bracken and over rock, smilingly, thankfully storing that treasured experience.

A love had been born and growing for the teacher in Bury and here a love of a different kind, a love of the Lakes, later to be shared with my heart's love.

Amidst all this beauty I accepted, coped with, almost enjoyed fiendish assault courses, crawled up slopes with live ammunition being fired over my head, with thunderflashes bursting around. The false horror could never diminish the beauty in my own mind of the whole area of sun, cloud, light, shade on hill, mountain, valley, stream and lake.

That varied emotional fortnight contained two extraordinary incidents. No, hardly incidents – more life-long moments. The first one occurred during part of an arranged exercise.

We were all taken, late one afternoon, to an area the other side of Ullswater, driven in lorries away from the valley, down the twisting, turning, steeply descending roadway, round the head of Ullswater to a pleasant field sloping up to lovely woodland and left there for the night to fend for ourselves, with the information that we would be collected up at 9 am the following day. We were given meagre food rations which included solid small blocks of oatmeal for morning porridge. Oh, and a warning – "Remember, an enemy may attack during the night!"

We – a squad of young would-be officers, settled down, having sorted out the rota of night watchmen. No enemy came. We awoke to a clear morning, soaked the oatmeal blocks in our water ration, heated it as best we could, swallowed it as best we could. To everyone that oatmeal seemed to swell and then harden like a plaster cast in our insides.

The campsite was duly tidied as the lorries returned. We clambered aboard and happily, thankfully, started to enjoy the drive back, round the head of the lake and turning to start the one-mile-an-hour, first gear drive up the Snake! The tailboard securely up, one half cut off the outside world so giving us the view behind and the fresh air to keep us awake for the day's work ahead. At first it was fresh air, but then, as the slow twists and turns followed unendingly one after another, a few faces were turning decidedly green. It was when exhaust fumes blew back into us that some felt visibly nauseous, longing to be rid of clogged half-cooked porridge. One poor fellow could stand it no longer, and leapt to the edge of the tailboard, leaned over, vomited, convulsed violently and to our horror, thinking he was attempting some wild suicidal escape, we tried to grab at him, but he was gone! We saw him running away down the road and our vehicle swung round the next turn. He was out of sight. Gone, gone for good? No! Next moment he came into view, running to catch up with the crawling vehicle.

Clambering back over the tailboard, he cried, "My teeth! I lost my teeth." He brandished them aloft in his fist in triumph. Roars of hysterical laughter followed and all ideas of sickness vanished.

The second lifelong moment was one which stirred a different emotion entirely, although only a few yards (or metres, if you must!) from the scene of Moment One.

About six of us had chosen to walk quietly exploring the valley head. We wandered around the fell-side away from the Nab and the bungalow. On the way back there is a little church, ancient, miniature, standing alone just off the narrow roadway. We walked across the small graveyard area, pushed open the west door and stood inside the silent, peaceful bare little quadrangle and looked eastwards at the altar dimly illuminated by the late afternoon light from the east window. My special friend and I moved forward to read some inscriptions on a tablet on the wall just to the right of the altar.

I heard a gentle noise behind me say, "Lovely church, isn't it?" We turned to see a figure behind us of a kind, clean-shaven faced man dressed in long, almost archaic black religious order. He told us about the church. We moved to the altar frontal and we stood listening to his gentle quiet voice. He paused. We turned to look up at the east window. There was silence. We turned round. There was no-one there. Two or three of our friends were looking at notices near the west entrance.

"Did anyone just go out?" I asked.

"No, we haven't seen anyone," came the reply, "But a gentleman has just been talking to us – surely?" I queried. They had seen no-one.

We all went outside and looked around the fellside, up the fells, down the roadway, up towards the campsite, and saw no human being, just us standing amazed, puzzled, wondering amongst the beauty of our surroundings.

I have never forgotten that moment, strange and haunting but full of peace, tranquillity and certainty. As I write, that fellside stays the same and will season after season with the ancient little church patiently waiting there to greet whoever will venture inside.

PASSPORT PHOTO 1943

11. PERSONAL BELONGINGS, COMMISSIONING AND MARRIAGE

Treasures in wartime seem to glow with light so much brighter, gathered and held for safe storage. Life in those days for me needed to be appreciated. It was held so often not by a strong line of wire or thick, thick rope, but so often by the thinness of string, dangerously weak.

I needed so much to have at hand not only my prayer book (handed to me by my parents' next door neighbour before I left for Dover Castle that day in August 1940 – I have it still, worn slightly and dirtied by continental mud) but also a small notebook in which I had over the months and years, copied out my favourite poems or short snippets of some novel. Poems mostly English but some French, even one or two poems I composed myself as I tried to express my love and aching longing to be with her. Elizabeth Barrett Browning's poem I read so often that I could say it at night as I strove for sleep to come.

"How do I love thee? Let me count the ways", or I would wake to recite Paul Verlaine

> *"Les sanglots longs*
> *Des violons*
> *De l'automne*
> *Blessent mon coeur*
> *D'une langueur Monotone."*

Wordsworth, Keats, Coleridge, Shakespeare I had them all collected in one little pocket notebook. My anthology – I have it still. Opposite the title page I have a little picture of English landscape by Rowland Hilder. But the cover on which I had a silhouette picture of soldiers in battle has long since withered and died. But the book itself remains old and safe.

To return to those OCTU days at Catterick, days of strain and high spirits. On the fells one day one fellow caught and tackled with a goat. Why I recall not, where exactly I recall less, but on return to our barracks, he stank of stinking goat. So we all stripped off his clothes and put them on the roof overnight in an attempt to make them and him smell the sweeter!

As the course neared its end, the captain who had guided us through the often gruelling weeks and months gave us all a pleasant pep-talk, congratulated us and as a farewell said, "It's quite likely I shall meet one or two of you again as I hand over an O.P. [Observation Post] to you in battle." But then came the passing out parade with regimental band and pomp and no room for circumstance. All went well. Special friend and I had asked to be posted to the same regiment. Our wish was granted and we joined the 13th H.A.C. (Honourable Artillery Company) Regt R.H.A. (Royal Horse Artillery) at Kilham, a village near to Driffield in Yorkshire, my friend Bob (Robert Lankesheer) and I, Graham, now at last a married man, married to Muriel (Muriel Talbot) at Brunswick Methodist Church 6 December 1943.

Wedding in uniform 6th December 1943

Preparing for D-Day

The artillery regiment consisted of three batteries, 'G', 'H' and 'I'. Bob was drafted to 'G' Battery, I to 'H' Battery.

Although some found the Major in command of 'H' Battery to be dauntingly, blusteringly over-powering with a 'don't-just-sit-there,-do-something' roar, I was happy with the security of his control.

The two of us – Bob and I – knew that we were both extra to the establishment of the regiment and there as replacement for officers who might fall seriously ill, badly wounded or even killed in action. The last mentioned was the unhoped-for eventuality. But we knew, having experienced training exercises and made acquaintances into friendships, that fate might take a hand in our future days.

Months went by – months which I enjoyed with new-found more serious responsibilities as a commissioned officer, and with my increasing respect for my Major. He had sent me on a T.E.W.T. (Training Exercise Without Troops) where many artillery officers in the 11th Armoured Division were gathered in a large hall, divided into several individual, walled cubicles, each with a long table set on one side, where there were piles of specially marked cards. With all watches synchronised, top brass commanders barked out orders for imaginary guns to start firing a great, lifting barrage. All changes for distance were to follow and each time I had to put up the correct card in full view of the high-ranking command. The day went well and I enjoyed it. On return to 'H' Battery, I had to report and explain the process to the Major.

A few weeks later this TEWT was repeated and the Major accompanied me, listening to orders and watching me putting up the cards. At one stage my hand hovered over the wrong card but quickly raised the correct one.

"I thought for a moment you were going to go wrong," he barked.

"I nearly did, sir!" I confessed and we both got the giggles together, relaxing as the exercise continued.

It was a moment of friendship.

The months went by, until news came through of an inspection parade. Who was coming? The answer was, "It couldn't be higher."

The morning came and the King and Queen together with Princesses Elizabeth and Margaret inspected us all on parade.

Later Montgomery came and spoke to us, easily and without pomp. The regiment was paraded in front of him, but before he started he said, "Break ranks and gather round me!" unexpectedly, but his speech of encouragement had so much more meaning and he gained so much more respect and confidence in his command.

All this meant that the planning of our invasion of France was well under way.

Waiting time

Bob and I together with other younger officers and men, all part of the reserve pool, were sent to Northiam in Kent to wait and wait. Having no idea how long it would be, we decided that we all needed some sort of exercise. We therefore devised a kind of route march with amusing clues demanding brains!

We planned routes with rhyming clues as a starting point and then across country others hidden in places hinted at before – yes, a Treasure Hunt! The final point would always be an inn or public house. It needed pre-planning. So Bob and I, on scrounged bicycles, would go off the day before to do the planting and chat with the landlord of the destination to ensure he was well armed to receive the thirsty men who would be arriving complete with their own food ration from base camp.

It was always enjoyable. I recall lying down in the grass by Bodiam Castle and watching in the summer warmth the smiling, laughing group coming up the slope and dashing off to find the next clue.

Looking back now, as I write, I wonder how many of them were able to survive the next incredible days, weeks, months. But then, in Kent, it was a few days of grasping at a moment of happiness.

A few days later, we were in the mess tent having our breakfast and listening to the radio. A hush, a sudden silence in the tent, as we listened to the expected, long-awaited, fateful news. Troops had landed in France. It was the sixth day of the month of June in the year 1944.

Five days later, we packed all our gear, with special food rations and specially printed notes of money to use in France, moved to Newhaven, boarded ship ready for the crossing of the Channel at dawn to reach Arromanches on D-Day plus 6.

Come with me. I shall try to put into words what I saw and what I felt on that amazing day.

12. INVASION

I awoke on board the thudding, tummy rumbling of the ship's engines and felt the slow, gentle movement out, free of the harbour's shelter, the breaking loose of links with Newhaven, Kent, England and my love.

Up on deck I watched the steady, careful drift past the Isle of Wight and the turn southwards out into the Channel, to feel the swell of the sea. I turned away from the receding coast of England and faced towards France and the Normandy coastline.

Bob joined me. It was a quiet early morning, a clear sky with slight early morning mist, two young lieutenants who knew they were moving away from safety out towards an incredible adventure, something momentous. We were part of history in the making.

We begged to be allowed on the captain's bridge. Permission was granted. Together we climbed to the tense area of command and gradually before us, beheld through the rectangular glass window the most extraordinary sight of clear water in front but either side anchored small vessels to which were tethered barrage balloons leaving a clear, wide passage through which, safe from dive bombers, ship after ship steamed onwards, all around us, moving inevitably to the coast of Normandy, a coastline which came nearer and clearer.

Bob turned to me, "But there's no sound track!" The window through which we were witnessing the most dramatic happening, was strangely not real. We both were sitting in a cinema. The window was a cinema screen.

I kept my astonished gaze on the scene and said, "It should be full orchestra with Rule Britannia!"

The vague coastline changed into a beach with the buildings, houses, hotels of Arromanches – a seaside town – and it was time to disembark. Strangely, differently, awkwardly we had to clamber over the ship's side down rope ladders on to an armoured, landing craft, several of which were gathered alongside. I got my men safely through the hatchway of one, as I stayed on the surface of the craft which was in constant movement with the swell of the waves. Many full vomit bags were handed up to me to be thrown overboard.

Beach landing 1944. 13 RHA gun landing on
Normandy beaches D-Day plus 8

I heard the sudden crash of explosions and saw a building on one side of the little town burst into smoke and rubble. I thought then that the place was being shelled but learnt later that much of the sea front of that place was having to be cleared to enable the great mass landing of future supplies. Glancing to my right I saw the first part of Mulberry Harbour was in place.

With crunch of the flat-bottomed craft, we were beached. We were quickly out of the craft, up the beach, through the town, on the way towards Bayeux to our designated field. The sun was out. We rested by the side of that road for a moment, exhausted in full pack.

Suddenly in open jeeps a few vehicles dashed towards us. In the leading vehicle sat a familiar figure, it was General Montgomery. Bob and I leapt to our feet, quickly saluted, with speed he replied with quick movement, and was gone towards Bayeux.

Later, that evening Bob and I walked into Bayeux, bought (with our special tricolour painted little franc notes) a bottle of white wine and a whole Camembert cheese. As the sun set, in that little precarious strip of Normandy beach-head, we drank wine and ate the soft cheese, filling our mouths and stomachs with the taste and smell of France. Bewildered perhaps but grateful that so far we had been safe, friendly, together in a foreign land.

A few days later, one of the officers of 'G' Battery was shaving himself early in the morning standing by the side of his armoured vehicle when fate stepped in hurling shrapnel at him. He fell snuffed out of his world, our lives, half shaven but with no necessity to complete the job. We both, Bob and I, knew him as a drinking friend at a local English pub. Bob was sent for, to replace him – an unenviably sad task.

Left behind, I now had sole responsibility for the group of men waiting in the reserve depot. One man confessed to me that he was suffering from venereal disease. Unlike the camps in England where there was always a special First Aid Toilet which included a tray or cabinet of special self-administrable anti-bacterial ointment, no such arrangement was available. Although in moving combat this was not to be expected, I thought it ought to be available at the reserve depot, and promised the fellow that I would see what could be done.

Walking around on my own, I chanced to see the colonel advancing towards me. I saluted. He paused to chat and asked me if there was anything that might give me cause for concern amongst the men. I took the opportunity to talk about the medical problem and wondered how many of the men were in the same health-threatening position. He agreed that the problem must be tackled.

Two days later, we met again and he asked me to consider foregoing a return to my artillery regiment and stay to help him. Thoughts of depot work, moving officers and men, receiving and sending all documentation. And then thought of my detailed, interesting learning of the art of gunnery – and of Bob and all my other friendships – I paused – thanked – but refused the offer. An unknown path had opened up with a bridgeway leading where? What if? What if?

But my call came – not to 'H' Battery, but to 'I' Battery. I rejoined the regiment one afternoon in June. The sun was setting. All was quiet on that Southern Front when gently, quietly, peacefully came the lovely sound of the playing of the Scottish pipes. It was a lone piper of the 51st Highlanders away to my right – on the west side of our area. I stood still that summer, golden evening, thinking of the strange, secure experience a kind of lull that comes before a storm.

Attack east of Caen

That storm came with a vengeance when, at about six o'clock in the morning came the droning sound, the deep pulsating hum of approaching heavy planes. The armoured artillery regiment had advanced over the one bridge over the river Orne for an attack by the 11th Armoured Division to form up east of Caen near the village of Ranville. The bridge, later to be named Pegasus Bridge with the little café on the western side was to be crossed to gain the region on the east side of Caen so enlarging the area obtained under our control so magnificently on D-Day by the parachute regiment. Orders from Monty were to get across the bridge but not on any account for any vehicle to attempt a return back. The attack must go ahead at all costs.

The drone of approaching bombers from various British airfields grew into an ear-hurting, drum-bursting beat. Moments later in front of my eyes I saw bomb, after bomb, after bomb explode, with an insistent earthquaking continual shudder, as grey-black clouds rose into the sky forming a wide arc of destruction.

We all gazed in awe as the scene grew and grew so near us, just ahead, a release of energy with such enormity, such power.

Orders were given that tanks, armoured half-tracks, all vehicles were to start up ready for the advance. We all knew our precise position to the mounted 25-pounder guns mounted on Sherman tank chassis. Mine was to the left side of 'I' Battery guns, ahead was to be the officer to be the observation post directing the gunfire as we advanced. My position on the extreme left had, on the left-hand side, woodland or a thick forested area. (I have the original map with my pencilled marking still.)

To my horror, the captain who was to be the observation post, rushed up to me crying:

"My tank won't start. My driver in error last night has put in water instead of petrol. What can we do?"

"Take mine. I'll stay to repair your tank as soon as possible." We exchanged teams and off he went into the mêlée of the attack.

Soon after, how long after I forget, whilst I was struggling to clear the engine of the disabled tank, my area came under attack. German aircraft swooped over the field of supplies, including great containers of petrol (and water).

I was standing up in an open tank as a plane dived low towards me, machine guns blasting away. I grasped the fixed repeating gun, raised it to fire but in that split second discovered elevation was impossible to lift it to aim at aircraft level. At the same moment, another larger plane dived towards me. In one frantic move, I jumped over the side to my left to drop my body into a trench. In mid-air I heard the crack of an exploding bomb and all the earth of that field seethed and heaved as in slow motion in front of me. I landed in a heap in the trench, strangely, miraculously untouched.

I did warn you at the beginning that I shouldn't really be here.

Having heaved myself up and safely out of the trench, I gazed around at the damaged scene. Petrol was exploding and bursting from a large lorry. Cries of the hurt, the lost, the dying filled the now darkening sky, the field now lit by burning vehicles. I gathered together as many of the men under my command as I could find. Taking them with me to a field away from the mayhem, we together took a quick roll call. Two men were missing.

"Right." I said, "You stay here. I'll go back and search for them. What are their Christian names?"

They told me and, even though there was the possibility of further attack, two stood up and offered to help.

The three of us went back calling them by name again and again. The search was unsuccessful. Fearing the worst we rejoined the others. I told them to settle down to sleep until daylight.

I lay there, suddenly recalling my near death experience. Several times I awoke jerking myself out of sleep to see again and again that earth screaming upwards in front of me.

Next morning, we again searched for the two missing colleagues. We found them, shell-shocked and badly shaken, with another group from another regiment. Although both shaken and stirred we had all survived.

Unable to go back over Pegasus Bridge, I searched around the area scrounging as much petrol as I could to refill the now cleaned petrol tank and the armoured tracked vehicle was alive and sound once more.

However, I heard then that my observation post officer had been wounded during that advance around Caen which, although some ground had been taken to enlarge, to some extent, our grip on the beachhead, it had not reached the originally planned success.

You can follow the route on the rear cover map.

13. IN THE BENY-BOCAGE AREA

Able now to re-cross the Orne, we were moved round westwards and then south through the Beny-Bocage area, not terribly good for tank movement and deployment of supporting self-propelled armoured 25-pounders. Quick surprise move was essential for success.

It was about this time that an urgent message came from 'G' Battery. My friend, Bob Lancasheer had suddenly collapsed and the Major there could do nothing with him.

I was taken to the area of 'G' Battery, not far away.

I found him lying on the ground, shaking, moaning, muttering emotionally, his hands holding and trembling, fiddling with cartridges and their container. I gently took them from him and handed it to one of his men who knelt by his side, helplessly, not knowing what to do with his deranged officer.

I was told briefly what had happened. Bob had ordered his sergeant to go down a road in his light armoured tracked vehicle with another of his men to meet up with the 'G' Battery guns. Bob had given him details of the wrong road and the sergeant with the other gunner had been ambushed and killed.

"I can't go on," sobbed Bob. "I killed them. I killed both of them."

I held both his shaking hands. His whole body was shaking with shock and shame. I tried hard to console him, putting the blame away from him, on to the unfortunate lack of communication in a fast-moving army in a difficult area. Such errors would be bound to occur.

Everything would have to be done but risks would have to be taken. Awful things would occur in the heat and danger of a moving war. I tried to reassure him and not bear the full, dreadful responsibility.

Slowly, slowly the shaking stopped and after a while I gently let go his hands, drew back, stood up, walked quietly away and returned to my time with 'I' Battery.

Meeting of Officers of 13th RHA. A blurred photo because of the slow speed in poor light but it is the only image I have of my dear friend Bob Lankesheer who is seated in front of me.

Moving out of the Bocage area, we turned eastwards, miles south of Caen and helped in our small way to close round the now-famous Falaise gap. Our break-out from that Normandy beach had begun and the Second Army with the 11th Armoured and the Guards Armoured divisions rattled, rolled and raced across France.

Break-out from Beach-head

As we trundled our way towards French villages and small towns, the grateful French lined our way with cheers and thanks. I recall passing slowly by the entrance to a nunnery. The big entrance door stood open and there stood a nun, perhaps the Mother Superior, I don't know, but she was there crying "Merci! Merci, beaucoup." hand raised as if in blessing, again and again to us all one by one.

Another time our hurried advance had caught a horse, being used by the Germans as a means of transporting carts of rations or light ammunition, in earlier shelling. The horse had been terribly injured and was struggling to get up. He lay there with one foreleg blown away. It was awful, cruel to watch the harrowing sight.

"Faites-le tuer!" several people in the crowd cried. Thinking like us, surely, they wanted it putting out of its misery. The officer behind me drew his revolver and quickly shot the poor animal in the head.

Out ran several men, brandishing large carving knives to cut the carcass up for the longed for supply of food for the whole village, whilst we drove away as speedily as possible. We were in France, a different culture.

On another occasion, during the rapid advance of 11th Armoured Division at night, I was in my half-track vehicle, straining my eyes to see the vehicle in front and to see exactly where we were going, when suddenly out of the darkness a hand shot into the vehicle's open side of the armoured door. A large arm grabbed around my neck, followed by an enormous bearded face and I was kissed brusquely, roughly and the grateful French resistance fighter was gone. Shock at first but then laughter from us all – my driver and crew included!

Break out 1944. Jubilation in industrial parts around Lens, south of Lille

I very often had the job of manning the O.P. (Observation Post) joining the infantry forward positions. A few weeks earlier, during a short rest period, the colonel had collected together his young officers to test their individual ability to order gunfire from O.P.s I was amongst them. Several went before me going forth with normal bracketing of his imagined moving target.

It came to my turn. I aimed to be different. I was given the idea of his moving target and imagined route. I spotted on his map a crossroads a few miles ahead. I ordered one gun into action, straddled the crossroads, got the target of the crossroads correct, when the colonel snapped, "What on earth are you doing?" He paused, looked at me, saw I was not shaken and said in calmer voice "Oh, I see! Carry on!" I ordered the gun to fire and all guns to record as target and waited until I and the colonel imagined the 'dream' enemy had just reached the target for me to order "Target No. 115." (or whatever!) "Fire!". I imagined destruction of surprised enemy! I felt smugly pleased and I think he was impressed.

The move to hospital

Anyway, I was in Belgium at an O.P. with an infantry regiment in a field with one or two old fruit trees. One field away was a farm building held by the Germans, just about three hundred metres away. Yes, it was as close as that. I had ordered some shelling on to that area.

Standing by my armoured vehicle I turned to the infantry officer to say something when I was startled by a small explosion as a something, possibly a mortar-bomb, hit the tree. At the same time my right leg shot outwards, jerked uncontrollably as I fell back into the fellow's arms.

"Goodness!" I said, "I've been hit."

It was then that I felt a pain in the back of my right knee. What followed was sheer melodrama. I must confess I made myself enjoy the theatrical moment.

I became aware of stretcher bearers, my trouser leg being cut, the wound to be temporarily dressed and then the carrying out of the field, onto the road as shells whined overhead. I said with all the drama I could manage:

"Don't worry. Put me down on the road. Dive into the ditch. I'll be all right!"

More shells overhead, they dived. I was all right. I knew I would be. I was taken to the forward medical dressing station. My Major came to see how I was. The medical officer started to examine my wound as another casualty was brought in beside me.

"This looks a bad one, Doc," said the Major. I turned to look. I saw a young man who was snoring strangely. He was unconscious. The back of his head had been broken open.

"Oh, God. See to him quickly! I'm all right!" I murmured and turned away.

63

Eventually, I was given the necessary first aid, together with strong antiseptic drugs (would it have been sulphonamide?) It may have saved my leg but the effect made me feel dreadful.

A long agonizing rickety drive followed back to Brussels. Getting out with the sick or slightly wounded men, medical staff immediately put me on a stretcher and I was placed in a ward in the officers' wing to lie rather painfully but thankfully to doze.

An operation soon followed and I was cleanly stitched up to repair. The following day the surgeon asked how the repair job felt.

"Rather as if someone were holding a red hot poker against the back of my knee."

He prescribed a dose of morphine to help me to sleep. I tried it. I turned over to face the wall at the side of my bed, closed my eyes, drifted to sleep watching row after row of china plates fly across quietly with wings diagonally from left to right. No more pain. Just spell-bound, drug-inflicted sleep!

Many injections of penicillin – quite experimental in those days – aided my recovery. One morning a couple of the nurses came to by bedside and asked if I had suffered a painful reaction to the overnight injection. In assuring them that all was well, I asked them why they were so concerned, and they told me that a gentleman in the next ward had become very ill and they suspected a fault in that batch. I have thought about that since. Was it that he was actually allergic to penicillin – an unknown factor in those days?

I received many visits from young ladies of Brussels who would burst into the ward bringing grapes, laughter and chatter – a delightful break from the humdrum days of rigid routine. But after each visit it would be time for the next check on temperature.

"Oh, dear!" moaned the nurse, "It's good of those girls to visit – but it shoots your readings up each time!"

In spite of those amusing hiccups, I was eventually discharged from hospital and moved to a large house, still in Brussels, which had been converted into a convalescent home to adjust in mind and body and to move into A1 fitness.

Quickly moving into that category, I was given two routes to take, either to be posted to some strange artillery regiment or to make my own way to my own one – 13th (HAC) Regt. RHA. I longed to get back amongst those I knew so well.

I found out their position and, initially, went to 'I' Battery. On arrival, the Major of 'H' Battery asked for me to join him. To my delight I was moved and spent most of the rest of the campaign under his immediate, secure and respected command. A month away and now back amongst those I had got to know in earlier months before in England and Scotland.

Holland 1944. Left to right;
Tony Smith, Myself, Norman Young, B.S.M. Wheeler

14. ADVANCE INTO GERMANY

Movement now from one position to the next was not so wildly hectic as we coped with the crossing of the rivers Maas (Meuse) and the Rhine. My team of six men worked our drill with clockwork speed and precision. Leaping from our half-track, which I named Habañera, we Spanish-danced our race across fields marked gun positions, took angles, map reading, saw them mounted, set up for action in as short a time as we could. Every move and calculation flowed in friendly unison.

It was only much later as we chatted together near the shores of the Baltic that they made a confession – and eased their consciences.

Throughout our travels across Europe, a general, welcoming, now-free public would wave in thankful greeting and push into our hands bottle after bottle of wonderful wines. My half-track always had an ample 'cellar'. My team confessed to me, so much later, that on one occasion as we started our accustomed drill, they saw me as usual lead the race out and off away from the half-track. One of the crew had drunk far too much wine. They bundled the semi-conscious link-pin out and pushed him under the half-track out of sight as they raced madly doubling up so efficiently that I was unaware of the misdemeanour. I, in that later time when we were an army of occupation, was able to laugh and congratulate them warmly for their brilliant quick thinking so preventing me from having to charge the poor fellow – a charge which would lead to possible serious punishment and a break-up of our otherwise perfect team.

Ambush and Danger
That team work came into its own one day as we were moving through Germany. It was another case of "I

really shouldn't be here" occasions. My fellow officer's half track was moving forward along our route of advance. I was following behind. Between us was an open-topped vehicle and our signals communicator on motorbike.

Quiet progress was suddenly shattered by a loud explosion by the side of the cyclist, who fell from his bike. I saw him sprawled in the roadway. My driver braked at once, as our radio spluttered into action. "You all right, Gra?" from the vehicle far in front. "Yes – it's signals!" I snapped as I opened my vehicle door to get out, shouting to two of my team, "You fire to the right, you take the left!" They gave me covering fire as I dashed to help the signaller to his feet. He collapsed with shock as I took him to bundle him into the back of the vehicle in front, shouting to the driver to move, move fast. I turned whilst covering fire continued, picked up the 500cc motor bike, hurled it into the side of the road, dashed to my vehicle and off we went. All this happened in the crammed chaos of about ten seconds.

I sank back into my seat. We moved out of the danger of an ambush. I thanked God that I had learnt my lesson on that late afternoon in Northern Ireland, that I had heard so often the maxim of my worshipped Major: "Don't just sit there. Do something!"

So many "I shouldn't-be-here" moments.

Once I was strolling with a fellow officer along the edge of a field, the hedge on our right and then, on the other side of that, the road. We chatted idly, admiring the view to our left. I could see a gap in the hedge ahead which would enable us to regain the road. Some white tape swung gently in the breeze, held safely to a post with some notice board at the top of the post. We continued slowly, peacefully forward towards that gap, the tape, that notice board, reached it, paused to read the notice. We read the bold, stark words: "Achtung! Minen!"

Yes, we had both walked through a minefield. What fates, what gods had guided us, I know not. Was it the answer to a prayer in a bluebell wood or on the top alone on a Cumbrian mountain?

So many narrow escapes! Once a shell landed on one side of a thick stone wall. I, on one side survived, protected. A young soldier on the other side was not and tragically did not.

I must tell you about what really was my most embarrassing moment, albeit a moment of solitary embarrassment.

I had displayed my guns in an advantageous field, with my half-track command post facing towards the guns in unorthodox arrangement. Behind me was a good-sized building with the guns able to fire over me and the building. This enabled me to be in safe control, knowing the men controlling the guns were fairly secure in their armoured tanks. The Germans that day were firing air-burst shells which sent scattered shrapnel from air to ground with deadly effect. Moderately safely ensconced in this manner, I settled down to await events. But my natural body functions suddenly required to be dealt with. My bowels urged me to take action. I pondered for a few moments. It would have been in breach of all army etiquette to dig my little hole and perform the natural act in front of the men. I knew I would have to go shovel in hand round, out of their sight, to the other side of the building where shells were bursting in the air at regular intervals. I waited. A shell whined, screamed, big ball of smoke in the air, thud of the explosion. Silence.

Armed with spade in one hand, toilet paper in the other, I ran the short distance in an arcing curve, hidden from view, dropped my khaki trousers and completed the very urgent need, bent down, started to pull up my trousers, and – scream, puff of smoke, crack of airborne explosion, the next shell exploded above me. I heard a loud, whoosh of sound, a strikingly large shaft of sharp steel flew in front of my head and embedded itself sharp point down into the ground, sharper point sticking at an angle up into the air right between my legs and my feet. Steam rose out of the soil from the hot metal. I still held on to my trousers and kept my feet planted apart, transfixed with horror. All I could murmur was, "Oh, dear! Oh, dear!". All I could think of, as a faint smile spread over my face, what an ignominious death it nearly was. That was a great - What if? What if?

I have taken you with me in imagination to the position of O.P. with forward infantry regiments. My vast treasure chest contains several, but two, I'm sure, will catch your interest.

The first was in December 1945, when I was ordered to go forward to a church in a German small town to relieve the O.P. which was being manned by an officer from another artillery regiment. I entered the church and climbed up, dark stone flight after flight of steps to the steeple top, reaching a small dark cold room with an open slit view out to fields in frosty, crackling winter bleakness. I looked out carefully and then turned to the officer waiting to give me details of the enemy's presence out across the darkening countryside. He started to speak quietly. I stopped him. He paused, looked at me. We changed names. Yes, it was the captain from Catterick Camp. The possible, the unlikely had occurred as he had predicted months, more than a year ago. He completed the necessary hand-over. We shook hands. He turned away and was gone, down, down and out of my life once more.

I have a book entitled "Taurus Pursuant – a history of the 11th Armoured Division", in which the last passages list all those who were killed in action. His name is not there I'm pleased to say.

The second O.P. incident escaping from my treasure chest concerns an all-night vigil with a different infantry regiment.

It was getting dark when my driver and gunner signaller arrived. After chattering with the infantry officer to grasp the full situation, to link this with my detailed map, the team and I settled down as comfortably as possible in the room of a small house that had been commandeered.

During the night, I was quickly asked to sit with the infantry officer. His forward guard, a few men outside had sent an urgent quiet message by his communication that they had heard voices to their right. Could I help? I looked at my map and I had marked on my map a target number at what I felt sure was the area, away near to the guard's position. I knew at once what I had to do. But I had never done such a gunnery drill before.

Wireless communication with my battery, alerted the artillery officer with the guns for action.

"Troop target! Close target. Target number 115, Gun No. 1. Fire!"

I waited, listened for the first shell to land. Heard the explosion. It sounded on target! "Gun No. 2,.Fire!" That sounded right, too. "Gun No. 3. Fire!" The whine of the shell. Explosion with dreadful crunch just to the right very near to me. "No. 3. Stand down." I was shaken, as I ordered No. 4. – the last – to fire, and that passed the test.

I ordered two rounds of gunfire from the three well-laid, correctly on target guns (as I hoped!), and all fell silent. The infantry officer thanked me and I left him to his vigil.

Five minutes later, I heard the infantry officer cry out, "Where's that gunner?" I dashed over to him, fearing the worst. "Well done! That was right. The men have just wired back. It was the exact spot!"

There was no further disturbance that night and my team and I drove away in the mist of early morning. I joined my fellow officers for breakfast and, I must admit, a stiff drink in gratitude. I had been forced to perform a complicated task, first time, with the right results. The team of No. 3 gun were justly reprimanded and later all were, because of that dangerous error, taught a worthwhile lesson.

So that memory slides back into its drawer.

*   *   *

15. THE HORROR OF WAR

But now, I must warn you I shall be talking of a memory that I dread to put into words. Can I possibly find the words to give the picture, the feeling, the personal depths of agony? What is to follow now, has haunted, cruelly, my mind. Dimmed perhaps, those other happier moments. Haunted me as did, so long, the smell of Normandy when tainted with burning buildings, fields aflame, cattle lying dead, swollen, split open in summer heat with long-remembered stench. But worse than that haunting, is, still is, what I am about to guide you through. Be warned.

One late afternoon, near K—ch, the guns were in action. My sergeant and I sat in control, in comfort, in a room of a small house, connected with each gun. I sat ordering the action, each gun controller responding with drill-precision.

As I concentrated carefully, a message came, quick and snapped unemotionally:

"Premature on Number One."

"Roger!" I accepted the message automatically. My sergeant said quietly "That'll be a mess!"

I turned. Time stopped. I repeated the word:

"Premature. Oh, my God!"

We both leapt to our feet. I quickly sent the news to headquarters and we fled from the room out to Number One's position. Together we climbed over the tracks and side of the open Sherman tank. No moving, living thing was there, I saw the large 25-pounder gun, glanced at several shells stacked ready for use, all smoking and steaming dangerously. One gunman was standing with a fire extinguisher. "Quick! Spray those shells at once!" He obeyed. I turned to the bombardier, crouched in his seat beside his direction instrument and leaning towards the barrel of the gun, unconscious, breathing strangely. I put my arms round him, one arm over his left side. I moved him gently and put my right hand to lift him out of his seat. My hand met no thigh but met a sharp, shattered spear of broken bone. With care, the sergeant and I lifted the poor fellow off his seat and lowered him over the side of the Sherman tank to the waiting men below. Of the two other men who made up the team, little complete was left. I kept handing pieces over to be sorted out on the ground. I shall never forget the moment I got hold of a leg and as I passed it over to a pair of willing hands,

"Take this. I don't know whose leg it is," I cried.

"I know, sir," came the reply, "it's T—'s." He spoke, kindly, reassuringly, tenderly as he put the limb on the appropriate pile.

Those men dug two temporary graves in the frosted ground and buried two separate groups – their comrades – their drinking pals – their battle-weary friends – so cruelly, so accidentally blown to pieces that winter afternoon.

Back in our command room, I told my sergeant that I wanted all of the men to meet together in a larger room of that empty house. Contacting my colonel I asked for my guns to be taken out of action for twenty minutes. Agreement came and my next painful task was to speak sensibly, carefully, helpfully.

My sergeant came, told me they were ready. He went before me, called them to attention. I thanked him, told them all to sit down. I paused, drew a deep breath, started. My exact words, oh, I can't recall them precisely.

I thanked all those who had helped with that dreadful clearance following the accident and then we all stood in silent prayer for the two now buried and for the third whom we knew would not survive. I remember I said a short prayer and then with the men seated, I had to tell them not to allow what had happened to affect them wrongly, weakly, but to strengthen them to work hard "to get this bloody war over as quickly and efficiently as possible". Yes, I remember using that word. We had gone far from the Normandy beaches, across France, Belgium, Holland, into Germany and the aim was to continue together.

Solemnly, we parted, out to continue our work.

Later, I had one more unwelcome task. I wanted to write, in my own hand, to the wives and family of the dead ones, giving no details, just saying "suddenly killed in action". To receive the dreadful news, not by War Office telegram, that cold machine printed message, but from the officer-in-command. Their replies which later reached me, showed sadness, much grief, but gratitude.

All this, at the age of twenty-five!

In lighter mood

Letter writing had to be part of my world throughout the campaign. Outward mail sometimes to my parents, more often to my beloved wife, all reassuring news without details, sent unsealed to be passed by censors. I serial numbered all my letters to M. Her letters often had messages for Bob. To amuse us both she invented a creature called Phrynee, a nymph of the woods who would send weird and wild messages in Lewis Carroll-like nonsense, to which we would both reply extending a silly, relaxing game. Goodness knows what the security censors thought of all this. Neither of us was questioned on the subject!

The 11th Armoured Division moved inevitably forward towards the shores of the Baltic. Behind us lay the hiccup of operation Market Garden of Arnhem and the bridge too far. I saw the gliders part from their taxi-like planes' power to sing through the air above me. I saw one lose balanced-glide and plunge crashing to earth. The sky seemed full of man-made birds.

Belsen Concentration Camp

Our advance led us past the gates of Belsen, the concentration camp which was rife with typhus. I passed the gates slowly and saw the Germans guarding it, beyond I saw huts and the camp. I never had the nightmare of visiting that disease, death-ridden interior. But a few weeks later, the officer in charge of the anti-aircraft defence of my position was drafted to go to help organise the clearance. He and I had gained a laughing, happy friendship. On his return from completing his unenviable task, I greeted him cheerfully.

"What was that job like? What did you have to do?" I asked innocently, unaware at that time of the conditions. He hung his head. No smile. No greeting.

"I can't. I can't!" he muttered.

Fearing that he had experienced something awful, I continued to probe sympathetically.

"Tell me. It might make you feel better."

He turned, walked from me, staggered to the edge of the field, bent slightly forward near the line of a hedge, alone, solitary and sobbed, sobbed and sobbed. I could only watch from a distance and gaze at the tragedy of a changed man, from laughing and joking to a man whose mind had been cruelly scarred by scenes that would surely stay with him for life.

I learned later about all the horrors of that camp Belsen, and only recently the fact that Anne Frank, whose diary now gives detail of her young, short life, died there a few days before I passed along the road with those closed gates.

It gave meaning to me, personally, that I was justified to be a small guilty cog in a huge killing machine.

16. RELAXATION

At brief moments of rest, withdrawn from battle forward, the Major would organise a party. Some empty house was used as an officers' mess. A large bowl was found, ready to be filled with an unholy mixture of wines, spirits and liqueurs to make what we called a punch. It was potent enough to give a kick and a punch! I announced proudly that my beloved had just informed me that I was to become a father.

"Congratulations, Gra," he roared. "We must have an even greater celebration." as he poured yet another draught of wine into the near-brimming bowl.

I can just about recall my faithful sergeant putting me on a sofa and covering me with a rug to sink into a deep, rather drunken sleep.

Next morning I arose bleary-eyed, dizzy and heavy-headed. My sergeant came to me with the news that the men were ready on parade outside and that they would all like their rifles to be inspected!

"Thank you, sergeant," I murmured, "I'll be out in a moment."

I knew the drill so well. It involved much loud stamping of the men's booted feet; the quick swinging of the rifle as I, in the drill, grasped the end of the rifle, jerk it quickly to my eyeball and peer down the barrel to see the gunner's thumbnail held at the correct angle at the other end near the butt of the rifle. This sends reflected light into the interior to prove all has been cleaned perfectly.

Right! Remember all that precision-drill. I went out, aware that this was a strangely unusual request and therefore a plot, a device to test my reactions. The sergeant brought them up to attention, loud order, heavy stamped response. He saluted me. I managed to reply as smartly as possible and turned to the first man. As I commenced the drill I caught the sign of an evil glint in that man's eye as he stamped a foot to allow me to grab and yank the top end of the rifle. So far, so good.

The next man could barely hide a controlled grin. Safely past him. No damage to my eye-ball. On and on. One after the other. I started grinning. They all started to shake with suppressed laughter.

I turned to my sergeant, and with great self-control said "Congratulate the men. A splendid turnout. Dismiss them, sergeant!" And we all broke ranks, laughing.

I had survived uninjured, appreciating the well-managed joke, which I knew had strengthened our relationship as a team.

Back on the move towards the Kiel canal and the Baltic, I was fatefully to see the last sight of my Major and his sergeant.

Last Months in Germany

A skirmish had occurred in the movement of advance. Some enemy shell-fire was heard. My driver swerved to one side of a tank which had halted, angled awkwardly across the roadway. One man lay on the road. I recognised him as the Major's sergeant.

"Stop." I ordered my driver and got out of my half-track, grasping from my pocket the tube packet of morphia, bent over the sergeant to find him unconscious, wounded but in no pain. I glanced up to the turret of the tank to see the Major half in, half out with his right arm hanging limply. Slowly, as if the film was running in slow motion, slowly, oh, so slowly, I realized I was looking up to see medics, and a medical officer holding something glinting, sharp in his hand, moving this instrument as he started amputating the mutilated arm. I turned away, horrified, went back to my vehicle, told the men what I had seen and we moved off shocked, stunned, silent.

I can look now today at the last pages of 'Taurus Pursuant' to the names of those killed in action in the section marked 13th RHA. Neither the Sergeant's name, nor the Major's appears in the list. So they survived. What has happened since? I often wonder.

Back though to the dash to the Baltic. We arrived, the three batteries G, H and I, on the north side of the canal within easy reach of the shores of the Baltic. Montgomery had accepted the surrender of the German army in that area signing taking place on Luneberg Heath.

Liaising with the displaced Polish people, we uncovered caches of German ammunition, swam in the Baltic, rested, searched houses for possible escapees from the Nazi hierarchy and some demonic scientific activity on the human race in one or other of the concentration camps.

Arrest of a German scientist

Quoting from the History of the 11th Armoured Division:

"On May 5th [1945] the official announcement was made that Field Marshall Montgomery had accepted the unconditional surrender of all German forces facing 21st Army Group. Total surrender did not follow until two days later. For us at any rate, the European war was over."

My regiment occupied the area Schleswig and Flensburg south of the frontier with Denmark. I had the job of going round the area talking to many displaced Polish men who helped me to uncover many secret piles of ammunition left by the Germans. We knew that the Russian army had advanced towards the Baltic but we had been given orders to get there first and that, should we come into contact with the Russians, we should greet them and whilst stopping their progress, stand firm engaging them with friendly conversation!

I did not meet the Russian army itself but one day I had to go with a Russian fellow to a house near Flensburg where a German scientist lived who, it was alleged, had committed atrocious cruelty in concentration camps following his work on the study of the fertilisation of infertile women.

The following gives details of his life and work. But - a serious warning - the details are gruesome.

Carl Clauberg (1898-1957)

Carl Clauberg was a medical doctor working in the gynaecological department Kiel University in Northern Germany and was later Professor of Gynaecology at the University of Königsberg. He was working on ways of helping infertile women to conceive. He joined the Nazi Party in 1933 and during the Second World War he asked Heinrich Himmler if he could carry out sterilisation experiments on large groups of women. His aim, in line with two goals of National Socialism, was to cure infertility in Aryan women and to prevent non-Aryans from reproducing by sterilising them whilst not affecting their ability to work. He was given permission and in December 1942 he moved to Auschwitz concentration camp. His laboratory was in part of Block number 10 in the main camp where he experimented with sterilizing both men and women using X-rays. Later he looked for a cheaper method and injected acid and other chemicals, such as formalin, into the uterus without anaesthetic. After several weeks, the fallopian tubes closed and remained blocked. He experimented mainly on Roma and Jewish women. Some of his subjects died as a result and others were killed in order for autopsies to be carried out. He was also reported to have carried out artificial insemination experiments. He wrote to Himmler in 1943, "The time is not far distant when I shall be able to say that one doctor, with, perhaps, ten assistants, can probably effect several hundred if not one thousand sterilisations in a single day."

When the Red Army approached Auschwitz he moved on to Ravensbrück concentration camp where he continued his research until he was captured in 1945.

In 1948 Clauberg was tried in the Soviet Union and was sentenced to 25 years in prison. However, after seven years, when there was an exchange of prisoners of war between the Soviet Union and West Germany, he was released and returned to West Germany where he boasted of his "scientific achievements". Groups of survivors protested and he was arrested in 1955 and put on trial but died of a heart attack in his prison cell before the trial.

The Russian, whose English was reasonably good, and I with my group of men, found the house and entered the premises. Whilst the Russian and I questioned the man, my men had quickly gone to the rear, entered and searched the house for any evidence. They rejoined us having found nothing. More questioning by the Russian produced no results. It was then that I noticed a briefcase leaning against the wall behind a chair. I picked it up, opened it and found a large number of sheets of foolscap clipped together – the papers filled with typed Germany script with the heading in German which I could easily and immediately translate – "The Fertilisation of Infertile Women".

The Russian and I arrested the doomed man to take him to H Battery where our newly appointed successor as Major had the task of looking at the evidence which I had found. The German scientist begged to be handed over to be sent to England for the inevitable trial. But it was the Russian official who had instigated the search and arrest and so, of course, it was his case, his criminal who had committed dreadful crimes in camps in the Russian area and we handed the scientist over. In 1948 he was tried and sentenced to 25 years in prison.

The Russian turned to me and thanked me for my "remarkable astuteness" – his words not mine!

 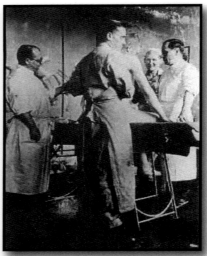

The Nazi physician Carl Clauberg (left), who performed medical experiments on prisoners in Block 10 of the Auschwitz camp (right).

Years later my wife and I visited Bletchley Park. During a pre-tour lecture we were told that much work was done during World War II in discovering the whereabouts of secret papers and documents and that the best place to hide anything was to leave it in the most obvious place virtually unhidden where no-one would think it worthwhile to look! How true that was in northern Germany in 1945.

17. LAST MONTHS IN THE ARMY

Eventually news came of my posting back to England. My wife had not been well and a compassionate posting had been granted.

On my last evening with 13th RHA I was invited to G Battery for a last meeting in Germany with Bob. We sat together going over our time together, listening to Mozart symphonies left behind in that pleasant German house. Time to go. Farewells done, my driver drove me out from the house, along the drive, to the guard post at the gate. The guard had been called out to salute me. My rank required just a butt-slapped salute. I was honoured to receive a full presentation of arms. Pleasurable, but emotional, too.

In England, I was posted to Didcot and became Officer in charge of barracks, later in charge of C Company with three pips – a captain.

My wife, with treatment, was getting better. Our first daughter was born in 1946. For a while, I stayed in the army.

One morning, the brigadier called all officers to his office of command. He was seeking suggestions on the problem of ensuring how the men could be kept in barracks especially overnight with a disciplinary order that would be both secure and acceptable by all non-commissioned ranks.

He explained the problem. We listened. There was a moment's pause. I spoke up and gave what I thought a satisfactory solution, putting the onus upon the men, regarding them as sensible, reasonably intelligent human beings. I forget the wording. The brigadier listened, remained quite still, pen raised on his desk paper.

"Was that all right, sir?" I asked.

"Yes, I agree with you. But I can't recall the exact wording."

"Oh, I'm so sorry, sir." I tried hard to repeat the suggestion word for word. He wrote, thanked us all and dismissed us.

Weeks later, he summoned me again to his room, this time on my own.

I saluted.

"Do sit down," he said. Removing my cap, I sat. He continued, "I'm recommending you for the post of adjutant to an artillery regiment, coastal defence in the Bahamas!"

I think I sat open-mouthed in amazement.

"Well now," he resumed, "will you accept it?"

"I am extremely grateful, sir, but please allow me time to discuss the matter with my wife."

"Certainly! Certainly! Just let me know what you decide to do."

I stood, replaced headgear, saluted, and left.

That evening we talked, my beloved and I. The Bahamas! It would mean a permanent position, a regular army posting, my going out first, alone and then to ask permission for my wife to move into the regimental area, married quarters, the social life, with the Duke and Duchess of Windsor there – and all I wanted was to teach in an England at peace.

As always, my wife and I were decisively in agreement. I, with polite, diplomatic words refused the offer.

A few days later, my sergeant came into my office.

"Excuse me, sir, but I have a group of men outside on parade. They are just off to be demobbed. Would you like to talk to them?"

"Indeed I would. I'll be out in a second!"
I went outside to thank them for all they had done throughout their service time and wished them all well. "I'll be joining you all in Civvie Street as well in two weeks' time!"

"Well done, sir! Good luck sir!" came their replies.

We shook hands – they all left. Two weeks later so did I.

I remember in regimental stores handing over amongst other things my revolver which had been with me across Europe. Removing it from the holster, I broke open the barrel and laid it open, proving it to be free of bullets on the Quartermaster's desk.

"Thank you, sir! How few officers follow that courtesy drill!" I thanked him, signed the necessary papers and left him, Didcot Barracks, the army to turn the pages of my life for the next chapter!

18. A TEACHER AT LAST

I applied for consideration to be accepted for full teacher training. After a short interview and a detailed reading of my C.V. – education, exam results, army experience, I was accepted, assured a place at a college near Swindon, but that I would have to wait about five months. I, therefore, to gain both experience and a few pounds to help our bank balance, applied for and got a post with Oxford Extra-Mural Studies Department to teach Poles the English language to ease their resettlement in Britain.

Then followed an intense, full-time residential college course to give me the necessary professional qualification to follow what I had always wanted – a teaching career.

Training College and first posts

I took English Language and Literature as my first subject, choosing for my thesis women writers in literature. I joined the Dramatic Society, had great fun acting in the three plays produced during the long course. They were Shaw's 'Androcles and the Lion', Auden and Isherwood's 'Ascent of K6', and 'Thunder Rock'. I was, I'm happy to say, also elected as president of the Society!

Teaching practices went delightfully and, although the course was residential, I was able to get several weekends to be with my wife and growing child, often taking two or three college friends with me.

My personal tutor, having to observe another student on teaching practice, close to our house, came to stay for a while. He came home one evening with a pile of leafed branches which he scattered over the hall floor. He called to my wife busy in the kitchen preparing an evening meal "Quick, come here. Help me name all these leaves. I've just seen the most awful lesson!" He knew that M's speciality (amongst many others!) was botany! Chaos as M. coped and pacified!

Muriel 1954

But enough! I must lead you quickly through the following years. I passed with happy flying colours and after a short time at a primary school where I had had a teaching practice, I applied for the post of English Language and Literature in the Secondary part of an all-age school. There I really cut my teeth, as it were. At all class levels I insisted on good speech, good handwriting, clear use of English and saturated them with poetry of all kinds, hurled Shakespeare at them from the age of eleven to fifteen – comedy, history, tragedy – they had the lot. I took the top classes to see wonderful productions of 'Othello' where glancing along my row of seats I saw girls in tears at the end, Michael Redgrave's 'Hamlet' – where I heard whispers, "He's really crying!" 'A Midsummer Night's Dream' where they roared with laughter at the Pyramus and Thisbe scene.

Myself aged 30. Botley All Age School

Giving readings and acting Shakespeare in class, I never needed to stop to explain meanings of words but granted them the intelligence and emotion to grasp all that was necessary. In 'Hamlet' there is a speech when the Prince expresses horror at the thought that his uncle has married and slept with his mother:

"To post with such dexterity to incestuous sheets."

I spat out those words "incestuous sheets" – and heard the class of secondary modern boys and girls gasp and shudder with disgust and amazement.

'The Merchant of Venice' was included in the packed syllabus. Once, during the scene in which Shylock holds the knife to cut the pound of flesh – "pound no less, no more," says Portia, I heard a thud and discovered one girl had fainted!

Third year pupils had a year's study of the growth of language and literature from Anglo-Saxon times to their present day including theatre and cinema development. They had the task of reproducing visual pictures to be secured to the wall all around the room following a date-line which had to reach the present time by the end of the summer term. Included, of course, was Chaucer. Once, when I was giving them the Prologue in Chaucerian language followed by Nevill Coghill's translation one boy burst out, in protest, "But it has lost all its music!" Thirteen years old, considered not very bright, well below grammar school standard. His criticism was so, so justified. I remember I paused to soak in his words and knew then that I must never, never underestimate the ability, the under-the-surface intelligence of any pupil of any age, and never accept any category under which anyone also has pigeon-placed that young human being!

As regards poetry I had included in my syllabus Coleridge's long poem 'The Rime of the Ancient Mariner'. Sometimes I was timetabled to have double periods, so I planned to give one class my reading of this poem complete without a pause. I gave a short synopsis of Coleridge and Wordsworth and their idea of producing mystical, haunting poems in a language and use of words that could be generally and easily understood. I knew that one boy in that class seemed to have very short concentration time, but had noticed occasionally he scribbled wildly on rough paper to control himself. So, before I started I gave him a blank sheet of foolscap and a pencil, said nothing but started to give them all the poem as dramatically as I could. After the thirty to thirty-five minutes came the lines

> 'A sadder and a wiser man,
> He rose the morrow morn.'

The boy whose behaviour might have ruined the atmosphere, flung down his pencil and looked up at me.

"Oh, sir," he exclaimed, "that was smashing!"

I glanced at his sheet of foolscap. It was filled with the most violent scribble, swirls and patterns covering every inch of the paper. Concentration had been nightmarishly extreme. He had had a wonderful experience and the whole class, as a result, had been swept away with the narrative so brilliantly created by the Romantic poet.

I always told my classes that poetry appreciation was a personal feeling. So my poetry syllabus was filled with a large number of all types of poems. My classroom cupboard was crammed with as many collections of books of poetry as I could. Each pupil was given a special exercise book to be entitled 'My Own Anthology' and they were told to copy into it only the poems which they found moved them personally. I allowed them to decorate the paper as they wished with drawings using pencil, colour, design as pleased them. They were promised that when filled to their liking their anthologies were to become their own property to be their personal poetic treasure.

Of course, I gave them time to laugh with little snippets such as:

> Gertie, with a quiet tread,
> Placed a bomb 'neath Auntie's bed,
> Then, with very decent feeling,
> Scraped her neatly off the ceiling!

The art of miming would catch the imagination of a class. I would mime something hilariously stupid and then pick on members of the class to describe in detail what I had been doing. This was followed by pupils performing a mime, perhaps suggested by me if necessary, followed by me picking a pupil to put into words the actions just performed. Combined then in one lesson was learning the art of mime followed by the act of speaking clearly and confidently to an audience using well-constructed sentences, learning with fun.

I started with all the secondary school classes in this school a Drama Club which met after school as well as one timetabled afternoon rehearsing plays which I carefully edited or plays which I wrote myself adapting novels such as 'Little Women' and 'What Katy Did'. They coped admirably with shortened versions of Shaw's 'Androcles and the Lion', 'Arms and the Man', 'St Joan'.

Later came the move to become Head of English at a comprehensive school and superintendent of Evening Classes. All very hard work and having now two daughters, with my beloved wife teaching full time, I longed to have a school of my own to create the atmosphere that I wanted to inculcate giving pleasure and laughter together with the satisfaction of reaching the highest possible standards.

My two daughters, Jennifer and Susan
in the front room at 6 Maple Close, Botley 1957

19. HEADSHIP

After several shortlisted interviews, I was appointed as Head of a small primary school in the village of Kingston Bagpuize which I knew was due to be expanded by the building of a large estate, so making it necessary to plan the building of a new school, and the appointment of extended teaching staff.

We moved into School House in 1960 after ten years experience in teaching – in a primary school, then an all-age school and then a secondary school. My wife and I with several log books written by earlier Heads sat reading, reading, musing over all the records of the past. We were so saturated with the lives, difficulties, successes that we felt haunted by their very presence as we crept up the stairs to bed!

The school building, erected in 1894 was on the west side of School House with the Village Hall on the east side. Two classes were in the main building with another in the Village Hall. School lunches were delivered and eaten in the Village Hall. It was an arrangement which worked reasonably well with school numbers at around sixty.

The "Old School" now the Scout HQ

Being a teaching head of a small school is hard work if one is determined to get the best out of each pupil in a class of 8-11 year olds. I was determined to ensure that each child should know by heart all times tables and their meaning. Some found it more difficult than others, of course. So I made it as much fun as possible and told them the rhyme I had myself learnt at the age of 8.

> "Eight eights are sixty four.
> Shut your gob and say no more!"

One day we were involved in Tables Test Time when in walked an H.M.I. (Her Majesty's Inspector). I greeted him and continued the twenty questions of the test. To ensure that no-one came out with a panic stricken nothing on a personal score sheet, I always included "Eight eights" – always greeted with laughter. The Inspector asked why laughter had occurred when I called out "Eight eights".

"Ah," I said, "they all know a wicked rhyme". I turned to the class of smiling children and told them to tell the visitor, using quiet voices, the happy mnemonic.

> "Eight eights are sixty four.
> Shut your gob and say no more" – sotto voce.

The Inspector roared with laughter and went away seemingly well pleased!

During those five years, I was able to organise with the help of staff and parents a coach trip for a day by the sea during the Summer Term. Armed with packed lunches (and swimming costumes) we would set out for Hayling Island. Amongst them at that time was one Romany boy. He had no swimming trunks and looked longingly at the others splashing about on the water's edge. One boy seeing his envious gaze, came out of the water and offered to lend him his trunks. After a quick change, he dashed in to enjoy the fun, but rose up from the sea, crying, "Ugh! Someone's put salt in it!" Explanations followed what was a wonderful first experience.

That same boy was brought to me later after being teased in the playground by others calling him "gypsy". I chatted quietly to him saying "You are a true Romany, aren't you?" I said. He nodded in silence. "Well, that is something that you must be very proud of. Please remember that always." He smiled and went back outside to play.

20. NEW SCHOOL BUILDING

Gradually, plans for the new estate were passed and road lay-out started, and building was under way. I kept in close contact with the man in charge of progress, so that planning of a new primary school on the site could keep pace with the growing demand of school places. The Director of Education for Berkshire had visited many times and I had to go several times to Reading to discuss the plans being drawn up by the County Architect. The Deputy Director and I would look carefully at the plans. The architect and I had talked together to ensure that what he wanted and my ideas coincided. The craze at the time was for completely open plan lay-out. This was what neither of us wanted – rather the reverse. I wanted five-year-olds to come into an enclosed room of their own but as they grew older seven, eight, nine, ten to eleven year olds would have rooms that could be opened up with joined spaces for craft work or library areas for research work. It was a tactical battle to get a satisfactory result.

For a few years all progressed well until a steel strike delayed the initial structure of the school. A portable classroom in the old school playground helped to ease the pressure of over-crowding. At that time of the early sixties I had to allow 1.5 primary school children per household. Therefore the estate manager and I calculated expected numbers to give the Education Authority constant updates of future expectations.

All this pre-planning enabled the building of the school to be completed in two stages. First stage would include administrative block, hall and four classrooms. Second stage would be two more classrooms.

As the school grew in pupil numbers more teachers needed to be appointed as well as kitchen staff with cook-in-charge plus helpers, school cleaner-in-charge plus helper with later a caretaker. Arrangements were made through Faringdon Evening Classes for evening classes to be held at the school. Parents were encouraged to help in many ways. They helped during the day to organise a large reference library and to raise funds for a swimming pool. Cost of running the pool, general maintenance and purification, together with cost of heating had to be met with special school funding. This was, at that time, a highly successful venture and every pupil learnt to swim with confidence before moving on to secondary school. Strict safety and hygiene regulations were observed, at a time when there were no E.U. rules!

*The school plaque made for the new school
by John Blandy*

There was a special opening ceremony for the school with parents, all the pupils, staff, dignitaries and John Blandy himself to unveil the plaque which he had made himself as a gift to the school.

Professor John Blandy looks at the plaque he designed for the opening of John Bandy School on 19th June 1968

Some days later the School was blessed at a special service performed by Church of England, Methodist and Roman Catholic ministers.

So from 1968 to 1980 the School progressed and grew just as I had planned with the basic English and Maths, plus Science, History, French, Arts and Crafts, Music, P.E. and Games in variety to allow for different skills, Club activities including specialised Needlework, Chess and Country Dancing, Recorder playing of Tenor, Treble and Descant.

Recorder players were able to play for the hymn singing at the daily Morning Assembly. Every Thursday I gave a special talk but on Fridays it was the turn of the pupils to give Friday recitals – singly or in groups – entirely voluntary but this often formed the basis for afternoon or evening public performances.

My Wonderful Staff 1980:

Top row (left to right) Carol Rollinson, Ann Preston, Derek Clements, Cynthia Wyton (office), Josie Harrison

Bottom row (l-r) Ruth Bryon, Amberley Clark, myself, Joan Weaving, Pam Barling

When pupils were entering and leaving the hall I would play a recording of some classical work – the same for the whole week with details of the composer, the record, the work on a large notice board in the hall. For the last week of term I would allow the top class, after listening to all the recordings to vote for their individual favourite. I insisted that everyone had personal likes and dislikes. So as individuals they gave each recording marks out of ten. Votes were cast and counted. Top favourite was always played during that last week of term.

Years later I, now in retirement, often hear from parents that their now grown-up offspring will suddenly say, on hearing some music,

"Oh, stop, listen. We had that music at John Blandy School!"

I hope, as that is said, it is with happy memories of a time of growing at the impressionable age of five to eleven in an atmosphere of security, laughter and the joy of learning and of personal achievement.

One day as I was walking round the classrooms a tiny boy came up to me walking from the Infant area and said, "Hallo, sir. You're feeling better today, aren't you." It was a statement of concern, not a question. I had had a bad back for a few days.

"Well, yes, thank you. I am."

"I knew it. I could hear you laughing right from the other end of the school!"

I laughed again with him but thinking perhaps he was informing me, diplomatically, that I had disturbed him from his work!

But it is another moment to treasure!

The new school on the Draycott Moor Estate

As I write, it is glorious, galumphtious growth-making springtime. Brilliant, bud-bursting, warm-welcoming sunshine. My house martins returned three days ago to their nest above my bedroom window. A lovely big buzzing bumble bee that has just flown into the room, demanding freedom! Success! He/She – well – it has flown out of the opened window – and into the gentle, late afternoon welcoming air. I have left my radio on in the other room, filling the house with soothing music. With all this magic outside and the sounds inside and my memories, I am never alone – not completely. I sold my car yesterday. Another chapter of my life finished finally. Strange feeling – as though scissors have cut another link with the past years. Not an easy thought – but I must live with it, and accept it.

Gillian Squire's cookery class – with Liz Woolley (left) and Debbie Reynolds (right) making little cakes called 'melting moments'.

21. ACHIEVEMENT

Back to my years as Head of a fast growing primary school. I would often stand alone in the School Hall with not another living soul in the building and say to myself

"How lucky I am to have just what I had always longed for. Lovely building, wonderful staff, with a most satisfying catchment area!"

Yes, I was doing what I had always longed to do, to create a place of learning where boys and girls could grow and develop in personal satisfaction amidst laughter and happiness.

Of course, there were moments of serious difficulty – overcoming problems, needing much sympathetic care: a child having to be told of a father being involved in a very serious road accident, even the death of a parent, or of a parent with a life-threatening disease. Other world-shattering effects of marriage breakdowns which would cause earthquakes to the child mind. There were parents to talk to, parents naturally worried about their child's development and behaviour.

I recall an interview with one mother to whom I praised her boy, a hard worker, pleasant and so helpful with others in his class. Her comment was "Are we talking about the same child? He's awful at home. Naughty, disobedient and unhelpful!"

I explained that growing children were often two different characters – one school person and one home person and felt sure the nicer person would come out in the end. I met her years later and my prediction had proved right. She thanked me when introducing me to the boy's – now young man's wife and their little off-spring!

One morning, not long after the official opening, a letter arrived at the school addressed to my wife at School House. We had recently moved into our own house in another part of the village. To my surprise, we had been invited to a garden party at Buckingham Palace! We both had a wonderful day, driving there in our car, suitably dressed for the occasion. Police, seeing my special sticker on the windscreen, swept us to a parking space on Constitution Hill. We walked through the crowds, through the open gates into the Palace, across the inner courtyard and then through rooms, slowly so as to look around us, out into the gardens, marquees on our left where we would have our tea and over to our right another large marquee for the Queen's family and special guests. We wandered round all the gardens together, including the camomile lawn.

When the Queen came out we were all ushered to form an area leaving a wide passageway for her to pass, with the Duke of Edinburgh, Prince Charles and the Princess Royal (Princess Anne as she was then). Prince Charles stopped close by us (we had managed to be right at the front of the line of other guests) and he paused to chat to a Roman Catholic priest. We overheard him ask an inappropriately delicate question which raised a moment of laughter but no reply!

As we moved around I watched the Queen seated having her tea and was amused to see her gently ease her feet out of her shoes to sit with bare feet beneath the table unseen by her immediate guests!

My brother (the middle one) who was working at the time for an advertising agency in Berkeley Square met us as we walked out of the Palace gates. Together, the three of us climbed into my car for the drive out of London to my parents' house on the Essex coast to relax for the weekend, after an unusual adventure – unusual and enjoyable – a treasured memory of a County award for work done by my wife and I for education.

Supervising children in the school swimming pool

22. TOWARDS RETIREMENT

The years went by so quickly – both of us in our fifties enjoying to the full the now serious responsibilities – M. as Deputy Head of a large comprehensive school, me as Head of a Group III Primary School plus close links with Further Education and various village organisations. As a result we both had many evening commitments in addition to hard working days. School holidays were often broken by needs to deal with school administration but we had short escape routes to a little cottage in the Lake District where we both relaxed to enjoy all-day walks on the Fells, ridge walking, climbing to the tops armed with Wainwright's Guides in all seasons – all weathers. It refreshed, rejuvenated both of us to greet the beginning of the next term!

Our Lake District family cottage

In our earlier years we had taken our two daughters for holidays by the sea with my parents, but in our 50s they had fledged and flown the nest whilst M. and I edged towards retirement. For myself, I knew that I had created something that I was able to regard as satisfactory, satisfying, complete. I knew my nicknames – in the army – first in the ranks it was "Copper Knob" – in the Officers' mess it was just "Gray" – in schools as their teacher or as their Headmaster it was "old Platypus" – the last never to me personally, of course, but I knew quietly it was well meant with a chuckle!

*   *   *

It is April, 2011 and another lovely warm, early spring evening. With a fresh film in my old camera, I have just been out to take a photograph of that "loveliest of trees" the flowering cherry full bloom shot with evening sunlight. At my age of 91, recovering from a minor stroke, I know I may never see it in all its glory again. I hope so. But I may not. So my old camera has secured the memory for me. Old it is. A younger generation tells me I should "Go digital". Maybe I should, but my cantankerous old mind links digital with the poisonous "Digitalis". Silly I know but old age resents change and often resists it unreasonably!

*   *   *

Special note: My previous reel of film has just come back beautifully developed but all printed the wrong way round – all the past reversed! Significant? Symbolic? Revengeful? Or just modern inefficiency? I wonder!

*   *   *

You must forgive these breaks in time sequences. Be warned, they may occur more frequently, but to return to what was to be my last term of teaching (and almost M's). It was Spring Term, 1980.

John Blandy School had been open to the public several times, entertaining the village "Good Companions Club" to old time music-hall and tea, a concert of Friday recital items arranged and presented by top class, a performance of 'Joseph and the Amazing Technicolour Dreamcoat' specially arranged for choir, narrators, recorders and percussion. But at the end of my last term one member of my teaching staff, after careful research wrote and produced a history of the village school from Victorian times to the present day. All plans and rehearsals were done out of my sight and hearing, craftily but highly successfully. All boys and girls were dressed "historically". Character studies of previous Heads were played by the older ones and one boy with similarly fair hair as mine played "Me" with my top group recorder players. But as the scene was set, he turned to the audience and announced that I should conduct the little orchestra – a delightful idea! The ending was a performance of the ending of 'Joseph' in which I spotted the grinning faces of some pupils who had already moved on to secondary schools. It was for me a wonderful experience, which is now part of my treasure chest.

Later, came the last day of my educational career, completing the last entry in the official log book, the receiving of gifts, the leaving of keys on my desk, to be guarded by my very efficient secretary and devoted school caretaker. Job done, chapter finished and home to retirement at the age of sixty. The month was April, the year 1980.

My beloved wife, six months younger than me, retired on her sixtieth birthday (June 18th) but stayed to see her Sixth Form students through to their Maths exams.

At her retirement ceremony, she too wanted laughter. Due to the size of the school this had to be performed twice. She had to receive her gift from the pupils in a

My recorder players

presentation from the Head Boy. He was a very tall six foot lad whilst M. was barely five feet tall. Therefore at the first ceremony she obtained a chair and stood on it to be face to face. At the second, she got hold of the pupil's head and pushed him down to a kneeling position! I wasn't there to see it, but she described it to me, and how it caused waves of laughter each time.

However, when at last all was over and we experienced the moment together to realize that for both of us, we would never again stand in front of a class of children as professional teachers. Never again! We had a moment of clinging to each other to weep. It was the end of thirty to forty years of doing the job which we had both loved.

*   *   *

23. EARLY YEARS OF RETIREMENT

Those first years of retirement were utterly bewildering. What we both found so strange was that there was no such thing as "timetable" for each day. Diaries needed no entry of evening school or parent meetings. Each day was blank.

We knew we had to create activities. M. took on voluntary work with a probation office in Wantage. We both took over the editorship if the village newspaper. I had been Churchwarden of the local church but gave that up when I retired. We regularly booked times to get up to the Lake District.

After one year, we both joined the Oxford branch of the University of the Third Age and quickly found ourselves helping officially with that organisation.

To vary our holidays, we went abroad first with groups of the U3A but later, with our own motor caravan, we explored France. Earlier we had gone with our younger daughter, husband and children to French gites. But on our own we went to Normandy and I saw once more the little towns and beaches of Arromanches. I gazed at the remains of Mulberry Harbour. I wandered around the museum as the smells of 1944 came back – cattle with stomachs split open stinking in that summer's heat, the stench of death and decay. But that was gone for ever, just nagging hints of the past. We visited Bayeux where Bob and I had bought cheese and wine. We walked round the display of the tapestry and then the large cemetery on the south side of Bayeux – so many, so many cared for graves with cross after cross after cross.

Again, what if? What if? Should I really be here, I thought, alive with just a wounded knee? I, who had from 1950 to 1980 thirty years of wondrous joy as husband, father and teacher. I who had seen so many, many woods filled with bluebells, so many glorious sunsets, so many mountain tops, experienced so much love, so much beauty.

Now, as I write, on my own, sun streaming through the window, lovely music issuing from my radio in the other room, I realize, even though I have to write a chapter or two more of some heartache, I realize how grateful I must be for all the truly miraculously good moments, days, months, years that I have so far described.

Having worked, lived to a strict timetable for so many years, it was weird, worrying, almost frightening to wake up so many times to look at diaries void of brain-testing engagements. Joining Oxford U3A was our salvation. I was asked very quickly to take on organising Special Interest Groups where members could meet to study history, foreign languages, play reading, philosophy, any subject. We both joined several groups and my beloved took on the task of Treasurer! So our diaries were filled happily with committee meetings, going to weekly lectures and exercising our brains with our special Interest Groups! I also went to nearby towns to help with establishing new U3As! Later I became Membership Secretary as the numbers in Oxford U3A rose from about forty-five to three hundred – plus a waiting list!

All of this activity was indeed our salvation. We could stand up and talk to, lecture to – no, not to youngsters any more - to retired friends. Yes, we got to know so many lovely friends – all as a result of U3A.

It had been for M. and me a rescue, a re-birth of interest in the search for knowledge and truth and I wanted to do all I could to help others to enjoy a worthwhile retirement.

*   *   *

Together in early retirement. Garden patio, Haydown.

But old age and loss of links go together. My two brothers alive and active when M. and I retired in 1980 now dead. My mother had died in 1976 at the age of 90. She had been looked after in the bungalow in the grounds of the school where my elder brother was now Headmaster – a lovely building on a large estate of lawns, woodland, swimming pool, tennis courts. Remember now the dates of birth of my brothers and mine. The eldest born 1915, the middle one born 1918 and me born 1920. So (I shall do the maths for you!) my brothers were sixty-two and sixty-five when I retired at sixty. I who wasn't expected to live through infancy!

But live I did! I lived to enjoy with my beloved many adventurous years of happy retirement as I have told you but there were darker moments. The younger of my brothers developed cancer of the bladder and prostate. Bad circulation resulted in the amputation of one leg and after too long an illness died at the age of 74. Many years later my elder brother developed cancer of the bowel, partially cured but it spread later to the brain and he died at the age of 85. His wife, almost my last link with that generation, died about five years later after a stroke.

Soon after that my beloved's behaviour became strange, different. She often in moments of panic, fear, said she could not see properly. Later I realized she had had a series of mini-strokes. She started the downhill horrors of vascular dementia. Driving back from the Lake District cottage she said, "Does Mother know we are coming? Have you told her?" All sense of time and years no longer existed for her. Our home was not "home". She would sort clothes to go to Bury in Lancashire to her mother long, so long since dead.

My darling looked the same person, but she wasn't. I was slowly, slowly, oh so slowly losing her. I could only weep as link by link she went farther and farther away. Carers came to help. I took her to a wonderful local care centre to relieve the stress upon me.

Finally, following medical advice and with the help of my daughters she went into a superb nursing home and was later admitted into hospital sinking into a coma.

That day I sat by her bedside holding her hand. Gently, lovingly her thumb stroked my hand until later even that movement ceased. My younger daughter and I had stayed with her from 4 a.m. until 5 p.m., quietly kissed her and slipped away.

That evening I sank into bed at 8 p.m. lost, shattered. At 8.20 I must have dropped into a deep, deep sleep, when suddenly I was woken somehow – wide, wide awake. I could see the whole bedroom in a light brighter than the small dim landing light. I sat up and said to all four walls, "She's gone. She's gone." I sank back, head on pillows and closed my eyes.

Five minutes later the bedside 'phone rang, breaking the silence of the room. It was my daughter.

"Dad!" my daughter's voice, "I've just had a phone call from the hospital. Mum has died."

"I know." I murmured.

"Oh, did they ring you too?"

"No, dear. I just knew – five minutes ago."

That's all. Just the date – 4th November, 2009.

Sixty-six years of magical, star-dusted wonder. I can sit here now describing the incredible moment of quiet peace when my beloved just gently, gently slipped away from me.

Great, great soul searching sadness but what a moment to place so high in my long list of treasures, sad but so perfect.

*　*　*

Cremation, church service of thanksgiving followed. The church was full of those connected with M's life – close family, friends, villagers, her two sisters, relations, school colleagues, as well as those who had helped nurse her in her last months.

Later, much later, her ashes were scattered in a cleft of a rock on the edge of a pathway just above the family Lake District cottage where together M. and I had had so many lovely breaks from the routine of life.

It is there that I would wish to join her when my time comes.

Peace.
Daughter, husband and dogs, after the scattering of Muriel's ashes in Red Dell, above our cottage.

24. LIVING ALONE

So, at home, alone and the deep, deep pain of the loss, I filled the house with music. Both daughters, suffering their loss too, did much to help. Neighbours, friends visited. Church did all possible to help ease those first few weeks. But oh, that first communion without her by my side was shatteringly soul destroying. Our last communion services together were in the nursing home when I guided her so gently, lovingly through the shortened service, that last one when she said all the words of the Lord's Prayer perfectly. The kind lady who had taken the service said to me afterwards "How wonderful! I've never heard her say that before here!"

But gradually the pain, though still there, has eased. It is just something, an odd word, waking after sleep to see a vacant chair expected in my semi conscious mind to contain a smiling vision of my loved one, on even the phone someone asks a necessary question.

"Tell me. What was the date of your marriage?"

Forgotten? No, no! Never! The 6th December, 1943! And I burst into uncontrollable sobs!

But those moments are getting fewer and I seek for alternative moments of enjoyment with many people, and so many activities!

There was U3A – the weekly lectures, the monthly Philosophy meetings where I continued taking my turn to present papers, always a joy because it demanded complete concentration to discuss seriously our search for knowledge and truth. Always so many questions and no complete answers!

25. PERSONAL WEAKNESS

It was in July, 2010 when something rather upset my equilibrium in a different way. I was getting my midday meal ready and decided a small bottle of wine would be pleasant! I had to bend down to a low cupboard where I stored a number of bottles. Drawing one after the other from the recesses of my "cellar", I kept thinking "Oh, I had forgotten about that wine – or that one – or that!" After I suppose a quarter of an hour I chose a small bottle of claret. I took it to the kitchen, put the bottle on the side, looked at the meal cooking away merrily, when I suddenly felt dizzy and fell backwards, neatly, carefully. I lay there for a moment, felt all right, moved my legs carefully, sat up, moved to sit on the staircase by the kitchen door, sat for a moment, stood up, felt fine! I had my meal. I went for a walk up the road to see to a neighbour's house, put his mail safely away inside, re-set their burglar alarm, came back home for a restful afternoon and evening.

Next morning I awoke feeling curiously unwell to realize finally that actually it was not the bending down that had made me dizzy as I thought, but I had had a slight stroke. After a few days in the main hospital, followed by eight weeks recuperating in a Cottage Hospital and my younger daughter's home, I was able to get back to my own house where, here I am – slight heaviness in my right leg, numbness in my right cheek, and numbness in my right hand, making hand-writing something approaching a scrawl. But I am grateful that I can still manage on my own, secure with an alarm button in case of emergency, key holders who can rush to help as necessary and so many who visit and take me out shopping, for coffee, to keep making sure to take me to all U3A activities.

All this fills my days, my life with a purpose. I must not drive any more. I have sold my car – a sad moment, but it had to be. I've told the Philosophy Group that my paper which I gave three months ago was to be my last and so I must pause to give you something from that paper.Just for now ponder on this thought:

"It is for the philosopher to show how the whole of things can emerge from the tiny seed of self."

26. COMMUNION WITH NATURE

The years, the decades of my life have passed one after the other. It is strange now for me to think so much about the passage of time. All those days from childhood to maturity, from work in London to army life, from my teaching career to retirement, from loss of wife, close relatives and friends to coping with old age, all those years from which I am able now to pluck those moments of well-cultured memory.

From all of those moments so many are connected to my emotional connection with a full appreciation of life and the natural world. Of course I have already told you about bluebell woods, about mountain tops. There has been so much.

One such moment was when I came home from work in John Blandy School. It was a glorious evening with the quiet line of sunset beyond the field and distant woodland. I walked down the road to sit on the stone wall of the field below our house, my back to the field, face to the west to enjoy the sunset. There was the plodding noise of an animal behind me, followed by the muzzle and head of my younger daughter's pony. Its head rested quietly over my left shoulder. I stroked his muzzle and sat for a long while as the sun slipped down on the distant horizon. It was quite magical.

Another such moment concerned the house martins which have been coming to nest and raise their young using the apex of our roof front and back. About ten years ago when our countryside was lush with insects, the house martins had successfully raised two broods at the front and two more at the back. It was in September that I was standing in the front garden which overlooks farmland, when I overheard the cheerful, chattering chirruping of the young house martins as they flew from the nests back and front and exercised with showing off swoops and whirls, twisting and turning. I stood quite still and tried hard to imitate their happy twittering. They grouped and flew back towards me. I remained still and chirped with them. They flew all round me and then off to the far end of the field, then back again closer round and round my head. This game went on and on, dancing round me and off again happily in swirls of excitement. There seemed to be some weird connection. Were they saying, "We'll be off soon. Thank you for having us. Come and join us!" I don't know! It was another moment of unexplained magic.

As I write at the moment just one pair has returned. As the days get warmer I hope for more. They make a mess on the patio below their nests as little ones are taught to turn round with tails hanging out over the rim of the rock-hard mud nest. A plop sound on the path below and a clean nest above! They are welcome. I wish them luck with their breeding again here. It will not be easy. Flies and all small insects are scarce in number.

This love of nature and deep appreciation of the wonder of the world from gazing at racing raindrops on a window pane, to bluebells in a sun-dappled wood or the awe-inspiring majesty of mountain summits – all this together with having experienced the most wondrous marriage imaginable – makes me so grateful, so thankful for everything.

I realize I repeat myself in my endeavour to find fresh words to underline my feelings, to express the depths of my emotions.

Years ago my beloved and I drove over to Badbury Hill at bluebell time. Having parked the car we walked round the woodland clump close to the car park and met a young lad with his dog – the lad in early teens, the dog still very puppyish. They were playing with a stick – throw, catch, fetch, throw, catch, fetch. We passed each other. Further on, we had walked to the western edge and paused to look eastwards over the bluebells through the trees and saw boy and dog, game over, running together happily through sunlight and shadow – a oneness of boy and pet dog. I thought of that moment in time for that boy on the edge of manhood. Would he be able to treasure that moment himself? Would he be able to cope with loss of and bereavement for his faithful pet?

When M. and I retired my older daughter gave us a puppy – a border collie – who was called Benjamin – full name if naughty – just Benjie when good! He developed

Benjie, our border collie

into a highly intelligent dog with the unnerving ability to guide us off the fell tops, even in a blizzard, safely back to our parked car. His favourite game involved tennis balls holding two in his mouth and "footballing" a third round the lawn.

Together with our eldest granddaughter we visited an S.S.S.I. area in connection with her studies. With Ben on a lead we meandered along pathway, wooden walkways over boggy parts, in and out whilst sketches were made and photographs taken. Work finished we turned round realizing that for mere humans retracing our steps with any certainty was going to be haphazard and hazardous. I told Ben to guide us back to the car. With unerring steps he led the way, twisting, turning, path, walkway, small bridges, left, right, straight forward until we were amazed to see the car park and our parked car! No difficulty! He accepted our thanks and praise with a few wags of his tail, obviously surprised at human weaknesses! He gave us such wonderful company and strangely emotional understanding as we coped with the earlier years of retirement.

Benjie is certainly there in a little drawer in my treasure chest.

It has been a gloriously sunny, unusually warm springtime. A few mornings ago I awoke to the distant quiet call of the cuckoo. It was early. Sunrise. I had time to lie still within the comfort of bed. Today I heard the chatter of hungry birds in the nest above my bedroom window. The first brood of house martins has hatched.

I have so much to be thankful for. Although alone in body, I am not alone in mind. I am for ever mindful of my treasured memories, now shared with you from the small child gazing at raindrops, growing taller to see the table at eye-level, happy school days, finding the joys of art and music, wartime, the miracle of married life and love, six years of army experience, thirty fulfilling years of teaching and so to retirement.

Adjustment to retirement, at first not easy, but then days, weeks, months got happily filled with voluntary work locally and further afield. But then the torment of my beloved as she slipped slowly away from me until that strange, gentle goodbye.

*   *   *

EPILOGUE

At the end of my last philosophy paper I quoted Fichte's words:

"The kind of philosophy one adopts depends on the sort of man one is."

The path, the road along which one travels in life depends so much on the ripple effect of happenings around us and one's own approach to these ripples which might sometimes be storm waves. As I have mentioned so often, there is always the question, "What if?" and the thought of the road untravelled.

I am now in my ninety-second year of life, and I repeat, I really should not be here!

What kind of philosopher am I? Right! For me, I confess, I shall remain a romantic idealist!

*   *   *

I must now turn the key and lock the treasure chest of my mind safely, securely. It has been wonderful for me to be able to share it with you, covering nine decades of my journey through life.

Muriel and me in 1955

SCHOOLS WHERE WE TAUGHT

Muriel:
East Ward Secondary, Bury, Lancs
Botley (All Age) School, Berks.
Matthew Arnold School, Cumnor, Oxon.
Larkmead Comprehensive, Abingdon, Oxon (Head of Maths then Senior Mistress)

Graham:
Littlemore (C of E) Primary, Oxford.
Botley (All Age) School, Berks.
Matthew Arnold School, Cumnor, Oxon. (Head of English Dept, Senior Master.)
John Blandy School, Kingston Bagpuize with Southmoor. (Headmaster 1960-1980)

EXTRACTS FROM PERSONAL ANTHOLOGY
– carried throughout the war

Anthology for battle

7 Dream Season
Then scatter, scatter leaves of the passing year,
Old month of burning joy mature and dear,
I wish you gone, gone with no regret;
I like your changing cloak, your mists, and yet
I see beyond a joy supreme, far dearer than this passing
Autumntide.

Though winter comes and Summer leaves are shed,
My heart is Spring and Winter slumbers fast in bed;
The trees will burst for me in fresh new life,
The land will wake in dreaming past all strife
Of war and death which cease to be when comes my dream
Springtide.

Come, come, my darling heart in Spring with me and find
What fills our hearts with joy supreme and glad, but mind
Though Winter lies around there blooms for us alone
A Spring which grows more dearly than she has ever done,
Ohl, come with me, my love, my only heart and be made bride.

Graham Platt (November 1943).

11 A wish for time to pass
The winds blow scattering away the year,
Oh, month of leaves aburning be quickly gone,
The trees shed tearfully gowns held dear;
Oh, time of mists maturing, be quickly gone.
Now hangs the smoke of the gardener's fire,
Oh, wind blow all away and have it done;
For I have a heart which waits entire,
To lay before my love, when the month is done.

Graham Platt (November 1943).

My true Love
A sonnet composed in combat

How far does Love, the true Love reach?
And what great chasms, rocks and sands
Does this Love, the true Love breach?
For o'er vast seas I touch your hands,
I feel your breath and scent your hair,
So stands my Love, my true Love there.
I pause to tell you things I've done,
Of what I saw and how we won
More ground that day; a friend who died
His body torn and flung apart,
Of how he fell and how he cried,
And how his anguish tore my heart.
I feel your fingers through my hair,
Then stands my Love, my true Love there.

Graham Platt (November 1944).

The first two poems were composed whilst at Catterick OCTU and the Sonnet was composed while on active service.

* * *

Part of the Platt Family Tree

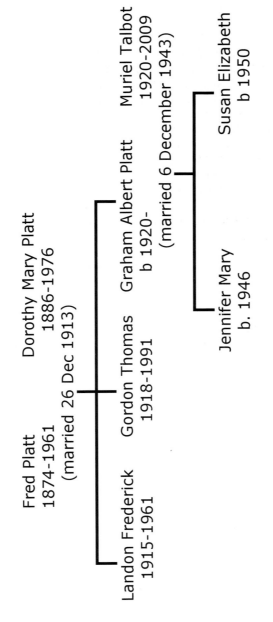

Fred Platt
1874-1961
(married 26 Dec 1913)

Dorothy Mary Platt
1886-1976

Landon Frederick
1915-1961

Gordon Thomas
1918-1991

Graham Albert Platt
b 1920-
(married 6 December 1943)

Muriel Talbot
1920-2009

Jennifer Mary
b. 1946

Susan Elizabeth
b 1950

1943   **2002**

Brunswick Church,
Bury, Lancashire

In the door of our
Lake District Cottage,
Coppermine, Coniston